MASTERING SPELLING

Barbara Seiger

CAMBRIDGE
THE ADULT EDUCATION COMPANY
New York • Toronto

Cambridge gratefully acknowledges the advice and contributions of the following adult educators who reviewed the draft version of this book:

Susan Adamowski, Assistant Dean, School of Continuing Education, Triton Community College, River Grove, Illinois

Marion E. Myers, Assistant Director of Programs for the Military—Atlantic Division, City Colleges of Chicago, Norfolk, Virginia

Stephen J. Steurer, Correctional Programs Specialist, National Institute for Corrections, Washington, D.C.

EXECUTIVE EDITOR: Brian Schenk
DEVELOPMENTAL EDITOR: Marjorie P. K. Weiser
PRODUCTION MANAGER: Arthur Michalez
MANAGING EDITOR: Eileen Guerrin

Cover Design by Richard Shen

Dictionary excerpts on pages 10, 15, 16, 17. With permission. From *Webster's New World Dictionary,* Second College Edition. Copyright © 1984 by Simon & Schuster, Inc.

Copyright © 1985 by Cambridge Book Company. **All rights reserved.** No part of this work covered by the copyrights hereon may be reproduced or used in any form or by any means—graphic, electronic, or mechanical, including photocopying, recording, or information storage and retrieval systems—without the written permission of the publisher. Manufactured in the United States of America.

ISBN 0-8428-0183-9

4 5 6 7 8 9

TABLE OF CONTENTS

TO THE READER   vi
TO THE INSTRUCTOR   viii

1. An Introduction to Spelling   1

How to Use This Book 1 / *What Is in This Book?* 2 /

2. Dictionary Skills   5

Finding Words in the Dictionary 5 / *Guide Words* 6 / Spelling Aids in Dictionary Entries 7 / *Pronunciation* 7 / *Syllables* 10 / *Accent Mark* 11 / *Part of Speech Labels* 12 / *Irregular Forms* 13 / *Homonyms* 14 / *Other Confusing Sound-Alikes* 14 / Other Information in Dictionary Entries 15 / *Definitions* 15 / *Synonyms and Antonyms* 16 / *Usage Labels* 16 / *Etymology* 17 / Exercises for Review 18 /

3. Spelling Rules   24

Pretest 24 / Rule One: *ie/ei* Words 26 / *Principal Exceptions to the ie/ei Rule* 26 / Rule Two: Words Ending in *y* 28 / Rule Three: Words Ending in Silent *e* 31 / *Principal Exceptions to the Silent e Rule* 33 / Rule Four: The Doubling Rule 35 / *One-Syllable Words and the Doubling Rule* 36 / *Words of More than One Syllable and the Doubling Rule* 39 / Rule Five: Words Ending in *c* 42 Exercises for Review 43 /

4. Forming Plurals   46

Pretest 46 / Rules for Forming Regular Plurals 47 / Rules for Forming Irregular Plurals 51 / Forming Plurals of Compound Words 55 / Exercises for Review 56 /

5. Contractions and Possessives   61

Pretest 61 / Contractions 62 / Possession 64 / Exercises for Review 68 /

6. Changing Forms of Words   72

Forming Nouns 73 / *Changing Adjectives to Nouns* 73 / *Changing Verbs to Nouns (and Nouns to Verbs)* 73 / *Changing Nouns to Another Noun Form* 75 / Forming Other Parts of Speech 76 / *Forming Adjectives* 76 / *Forming Adverbs* 77 / *Changing Verbs to Other Word Forms* 78 / The Adjective Forms of Geographical Names 79 / Using Prefixes to Form Antonyms 80 / Exercises for Review 82 /

7. Problems with Prefixes and Hyphens   85

Spellings and Uses of Common Prefixes 85 / *The Prefixes pre- and per-* 85 / *The Prefixes for- and fore-* 86 / *The Prefix dis-* 86 / *The Prefix de-* 87 / *The -sede, -ceed, and -cede Words* 88 / Forming Compound Words 89 / Exercises for Review 91 /

8. Pronunciation Helps and Hindrances   94

Commonly Mispronounced Words 94 / Sound-Alikes That Are Spelled Differently 95 / Letter Combinations That Are Pronounced Differently 97 / Silent Letters 98 / Exercises for Review 99 /

9. Homonyms   102

The Most Commonly Confused Words 92 / A Reference List of Commonly Used Homonyms 103 / And Some Near-Homonyms 119 / Exercises for Review 123 /

10. Capitalization   129

Rules for Firsts 129 / *Titles and Poetry* 130 / *Letter-Writing* 130 / Rules for Particular People 131 / *The Deity* 131 / *Names and Titles* 132 / *Names of Groups* 133 / Rules for

Places and Things 134 / *Places (on Earth and Otherwise)* 134 / *Organizations* 135 / *School Subjects and Printed Matter* 136 / Rules for Times and Events 137 / *Days, Months, and Holidays* 137 / *Special Occasions* 138 / Exercises for Review 138 /

11. Abbreviations 142

Abbreviations of Names and Titles 142 / *Titles of Respect* 142 / *Titles and Degrees after Names* 143 / *Company Names* 143 / Places and Times 144 / *Geographical Terms* 144 / *Addresses* 146 / *Days and Months* 146 / *Time, Numbers, and Dates* 147 / Commonly Used Abbreviations 148 / *Customary Measurement Terms* 148 / *Measures of Weight and Capacity* 148 / *Metric Measurement* 148 / *Abbreviations Used in Dictionary Entries* 149 / *Abbreviations for Charts and Business* 150 / *Publishing and Scholarly Abbreviations* 150 / *Some Other Familiar Abbreviations* 152 / Acronyms 153 / *Organization Names and Other Well-Known Acronyms* 153 / *Some Commonly Used Computer Acronyms* 154 / Exercises for Review 155 /

12. Spelling Lists 159

British and American Spelling 160 / Four Special Spelling Lists 161 / *The Arts* 161 / *Science and Technology* 162 / *Business* 162 / *Politics and Government* 163 / The Most Difficult Words to Spell 164 / *Double Trouble* 164 / *The Problem Words* 164 /

13. Mastery Tests 168

I. Mixed Mastery 168 / II. Word Groups 171 / III. Dictations 179 /

Index 190

TO THE READER

"Does spelling count?" How often has that question been asked when a written work was assigned? Some instructors may have answered "no." If so, they did you a disservice. In real life, spelling counts. At work, in your social life, in the community—anything you write represents you. Whether you send a report to the supervisor of your division at work, a letter to a friend, or a complaint to your local consumer organization, your written work will get the attention you want it to get only if it is clearly stated, neat, and *spelled correctly*. Incorrect spelling is the mark of a careless person.

Spelling is not an impossible skill to learn. It does not demand the highest levels of academic ability. But it *does* require time and attention. This book is designed to help you every step of the way. It will explain the rules, and the exceptions, clearly. It will give you time to practice each new spelling skill before teaching you the next. You will find yourself learning new things about words as you go. This will help you use words more effectively as you learn to spell them correctly.

In Chapter 1 you get started, learning why spelling is important and how this book can help you learn more about it. In Chapter 2 you will find out the many ways in which the dictionary can help you to improve your spelling. In Chapter 3 the basic spelling rules are presented, and numerous exercises give you a chance to practice each one. Chapters 4 through 7 help you solve some common spelling confusions; again, exercises throughout each chapter give you practice before you move on to learn the next topic.

Chapter 8 will improve your speaking at the same time as it improves your spelling, by showing you how careful pronunciation connects to correct spelling. Chapters 9 through 11 deal with special problems—homonyms, capitalization, and abbreviations—that are related to spelling. In Chapter 12 you will find several lists of words spelled correctly—words that you will find if you read about or are interested in science, art, government, and the world of business. There is also a long list of problem words—the ones that people most often spell incorrectly. If you study these words, you will expand your vocabulary and improve your spelling at the same time. You can use these lists to test yourself. Chapter 12 also gives you suggestions for ways to find words that are spelling problems for you, and how to overcome them.

Chapter 13 has tests in different formats, so you can test yourself at various stages in your study of spelling to see if you have improved. If you are using this book under the guidance of an instructor, your instructor will tell you how to use these tests. Otherwise, you may want to have a friend help you by reading some of them while you write the answers.

Remember, spelling counts. This book will make it count for you.

TO THE INSTRUCTOR

This book is designed to be used either in a classroom setting or for individual study. In Chapters 2 through 11, there are frequent exercises to reinforce the instruction, and a set of Exercises for Review at the end of the chapter. Pretests appear in several chapters, as appropriate to the subject. In addition, there is an entire chapter of Mastery Tests, presenting several ways to determine spelling capability. All of these test formats give you great flexibility in designing programs to meet your students' needs. In the absence of a Chapter Pretest, you may want to use selected exercises from the end-of-chapter "Exercises for Review" as pre-instruction diagnostics, reserving the remainder for Posttest use to make sure the chapter content has been learned.

Instruction has been broken down into individual modules discussing each rule, exception, or issue. Particular emphasis has been placed on showing students the patterns in the language, for when the student is sensitized to these, correct spelling is likely to follow. Lists to make learning easier are everywhere: There are lists of rules, lists of homonyms and near-homonyms, lists of abbreviations according to the subject area, and an up-to-the-minute list of computer acronyms. There are lists of words that constitute the familiar vocabulary of special areas of interest—science, business, the arts, government. There is a long list of words people are most likely to find troublesome to spell. All of these features have been designed to aid student retention of correct spelling, and to give you flexibility in adapting this text to the instructional method that is optimal for your students.

A separate Answer Key is arranged in the same sequence as the exercises in this book, making the answers easy to locate for learner and instructor alike. Cambridge, The Adult Education Company, hopes you and your students will enjoy using this book.

1. AN INTRODUCTION TO SPELLING

You finally saw that special someone you want to meet. But you're shy. And after a week of exchanging glances at the bus stop, it's obvious that your special person is shy, too. What should you do?

If talking is difficult, how about writing a letter?

After thinking about it for an evening, here's what you come up with:

Dere Intrasting Looking Person,

    I sawe you evry day this weak waiting for the bus. Im the one with the noospaper in front of my faze. Id like to meat you. Wood you like to take a wawk during your lunch our? You get of the stop before me so I now we work in the same nayborhood. If you are intrasted plese let me now.

p.s. if your marreed through this away!

You slip the note to that special person and you wait. And you wait some more. You're still waiting. As a matter of fact, you're also still waiting for that promotion and raise you expected six months ago.

Think what might have happened to your love life and your career if you had known how to spell!

Okay, that's the bad news. But there's good news, too. This spelling book will help you learn how to spell so you can go for that raise again (as well as the attractive someone who just moved into your building). But before you get started, here are some suggestions for making the best use of this text.

How to Use This Book

You can begin with Chapter 2 and go straight through to Chapter 13. Or, since each chapter is an independent unit, you can do the chapters in any order you like. But be sure to do them ALL!

Chapters 2 through 12 present learning objectives to tell you in advance what you will learn in the pages that follow. After you have completed the work in each chapter, look again at the learning objectives with which the chapter began. Did you learn the skills listed there? If you feel shaky on any topic, go back and review it before going on to the next chapter.

Within each chapter, the important concepts of that chapter's subject are explained. Explanations are clear, rules are brief, and examples are used to demonstrate the concept. Exceptions are given, too. The discussion of each spelling concept is followed by a brief set of exercises to help you test your own learning.

Each chapter ends with review exercises that also make sure you have learned the lessons of the chapter. And the last chapter in the book will give you even more practice through the mastery exercises. Check all your answers in the separate Answer Key.

This spelling book is designed so that you can either work independently or with the guidance of an instructor. However, if you do work by yourself, you may occasionally want to ask someone to read an exercise or list of words to you. The Answer Key contains the answers to all the exercises so you can check your own written work by yourself.

It's a good idea to keep your own spelling notebook. In it you can list all the words that are spelling challenges as you read or hear them. Look them up in a dictionary and write down the correct spellings. You may also want to list the words you use in conversation but are afraid to write because you're not sure how they're spelled.

Review your spelling list often, and keep it current by removing words you know and adding new ones you don't know. Keep your spelling notebook going FOREVER and you'll be the best speller on the block.

What Is in This Book?

How can you find a word in the dictionary if you don't know how to spell it? Chapter 2 answers this age-old question. You'll also learn about the ways in which the dictionary can help you develop spelling skills.

Did you know that there are only five basic rules of spelling? You'll find them in Chapter 3. Once you know these—and their exceptions—you'll have no trouble with 90 percent of the words you come across!

Do you know whether the correct plural is *heroes* or *heros, flies* or *flys, sons-in-law* or *son-in-laws?* You will find out in Chapter 4.

Chapter 5 will help you with one of the most common spelling mistakes: writing *it's* instead of *its*. This chapter will show you the correct uses of the apostrophe.

Chapter 6 will show you how words change—from *compete* to *competition;* from *music* to *musician;* from *happy* to *unhappy*. It will teach you how to spell the changed forms.

In Chapter 7 you'll see how to avoid spelling mistakes when writing words with prefixes and suffixes. You'll also find out about some spelling differences between American English and British English words.

Chapter 8 reviews some words that are often mispronounced, and misspelled as a result.

Chapter 9 is all about homonyms—words that sound alike but which have different spellings and meanings. There are so (sew?) many homonyms in the English language that the list is practically out of sight (cite?).

Chapter 10 is all about capital letters—when and how to use them. Chapter 11 does the same for abbreviations. It also contains lists of abbreviations for continued reference.

Chapter 12 contains lists of words people often misspell. Some may be problems for you, too. But they won't be after you study this chapter!

Chapter 13 contains mastery examinations. You're allowed as many wrong answers as you like—the first time around, that is. Then go back and study your mistakes. After that, your score should improve dramatically. Try to compete with yourself and give yourself a reward each time your score is higher.

Spelling well is a skill that brings rewards. In your personal life and in your career, you will often have to write—and you are judged by what you write. If you are a student, you know how important spelling is for papers and reports, and even for the note to the instructor explaining why you had to miss a class last week.

In the working world, almost every job and every business requires some writing. You may have to send memos, write letters, take messages, give instructions, or keep records. Accurate spelling is particularly important if you use a computer. Faulty spelling will cause your program to come to a halt. Who wants to see "SYNTAX ERROR" on the screen all the time? In the Age of Information, clear and correct communication is essential for success.

Then there's your private life. Chances are you have writing to do to run your household and keep up with friends. You must leave notes for family members, and jot down private thoughts to yourself, send greeting cards on special occasions and letters or postcards when you or others are away.

Whatever people do, they are constantly expressing ideas and feelings to each other and to themselves. When you handle language correctly, everything you write tells your reader that you are a careful, aware person who must be taken seriously. When you are able to spell correctly, you will feel confident enough to put more of your ideas and feelings on paper.

The ability to spell will not solve all career and personal problems by itself. But the experience of good spellers shows that good spelling eliminates a surprising number of stumbling blocks that keep people from being all they can be.

Now it's time to get to work.

2. DICTIONARY SKILLS

In this chapter you will learn:

1. how to find a word in the dictionary
2. how to pronounce words so you can spell them correctly
3. what information about words you can find in a dictionary

The dictionary is the basic guide to correct spelling. This chapter examines the ways in which a dictionary will help you spell. Some of the other things the dictionary can tell you will be summarized too. This chapter will refer to *Webster's New World Dictionary, Second College Edition*. However, you can use any standard desk or collegiate dictionary. You *will* need a dictionary for most of the exercises in this chapter.

FINDING WORDS IN THE DICTIONARY

All entry words in the dictionary are alphabetized. That is, they are listed in alphabetical order, or alphabetically. Words that have the same first letter are listed alphabetically according to the second letter. Words with the same first and second letters are listed alphabetically according to the third letter, and so on. The following words are listed alphabetically:

>pain
>pained
>painful

Word combinations are listed alphabetically as if they were one word:

>flying fox
>flying frog
>flying jib
>flying start

6 / Mastering Spelling

EXERCISE 1: Arrange the words in each column in alphabetical order.

A	B
tennis	art
golf	arrow
handball	ardor
baseball	ardent
swimming	archangel
snorkeling	artful
rugby	arrive
fencing	area code
skiing	article
racquetball	arbor

Guide Words

Each page of the dictionary has two guide words at the top. The guide word on the left is the first word on the page. The guide word on the right is the last word on the page. Every word on that page comes in alphabetical order between the two guide words.

EXERCISE 2: In each group, the words at the top are guide words from a dictionary page. Underline the words listed below that would appear on the dictionary page under the given guide words.

follower   **foolhardy**

following   fond   foolish
follow-up   foot   fondness
follows   folk   food

jean   **jerk**

jelly roll   jeremiad   jealous
Jebel Druze   jersey   jelly fish
Jekyll   jet-black   jeers

SPELLING AIDS IN DICTIONARY ENTRIES

Knowing how to pronounce a word correctly will help you spell it correctly. Incorrect pronunciation inevitably leads to incorrect spelling. Note the correct pronunciation of the following words.

ask   (*not* aks)
escape   (*not* excape)
February   (*not* Febuary)
entrance   (*not* enterance)
athletic   (*not* athaletic)
height   (*not* heighth)
perspiration   (*not* prespiration)
nuclear   (*not* nucular)

The dictionary helps you spell each word correctly by providing the correct pronunciation, syllable by syllable, and by indicating which syllable is stressed.

Pronunciation

The bold-faced word at the beginning of a dictionary entry gives you the correct spelling of the word. The dictionary then tells you how to pronounce the word by respelling it as it is pronounced. Because several letters or letter combinations can be pronounced in more than one way in English, the dictionary uses special letters and other symbols called **diacritical marks.** Each diacritical mark represents one particular sound of one letter or letter combination.

Pronunciation Guide

Diacritical marks are described in the pronunciation guide in the front of every dictionary. A short key is reproduced on the bottom of each page or on alternate pages. You do not need to be able to use these marks yourself to indicate pronunciation. But you should become familiar with the pronunciation key in your dictionary so you will know how to pronounce the words you look up. Always pronounce the symbol as it is described in the pronunciation guide words.

Symbol	Key Words	Symbol	Key Words
a	*a*sp, f*a*t, p*a*rrot	b	*b*ed, fa*b*le, du*b*
ā	*a*pe, d*a*te, pl*a*y	d	*d*ip, bea*d*le, ha*d*
ä	*a*h, c*a*r, f*a*ther	f	*f*all, a*f*ter, of*f*
		g	*g*et, ha*gg*le, do*g*
e	*e*lf, t*e*n, b*e*rry	h	*h*e, a*h*ead, *h*otel
ē	*e*ven, m*ee*t, mon*e*y	j	*j*oy, a*g*ile, ba*dg*e
		k	*k*ill, ta*ck*le, ba*k*e
i	*i*s, h*i*t, m*i*rror	l	*l*et, ye*ll*ow, ba*ll*
ī	*i*ce, b*i*te, h*i*gh	m	*m*et, ca*m*el, tri*m*
		n	*n*ot, fla*nn*el, to*n*
ō	*o*pen, t*o*ne, g*o*	p	*p*ut, a*pp*le, ta*p*
ô	*a*ll, h*o*rn, l*aw*	r	*r*ed, po*r*t, dea*r*
o͞o	*oo*ze, t*oo*l, cr*ew*	s	*s*ell, ca*s*tle, pa*ss*
oo	l*oo*k, p*u*ll, m*oo*r	t	*t*op, ca*tt*le, ha*t*
yo͞o	*u*se, c*u*te, f*ew*	v	*v*at, ho*v*el, ha*v*e
		w	*w*ill, al*w*ays, s*w*ear
oi	*oi*l, p*oi*nt, t*oy*	y	*y*et, on*i*on, *y*ard
ou	*ou*t, cr*ow*d, pl*ow*	z	*z*ebra, da*zz*le, ha*z*e
u	*u*p, c*u*t, c*o*lor	ch	*ch*in, cat*ch*er, ar*ch*
ur	*ur*n, f*ur*, det*er*	sh	*sh*e, cu*sh*ion, da*sh*
		th	*th*in, no*th*ing, tru*th*
ə	a in *a*go		
	e in ag*e*nt	*th*	*th*en, fa*th*er, la*th*e
	i in san*i*ty	zh	a*z*ure, lei*s*ure
	o in c*o*mply	ŋ	ri*ng*, a*n*ger, dri*n*k
	u in foc*u*s		
ər	p*er*haps, mur*der*		

Vowel Sounds

There are five vowels in English—*a, e, i, o, u*. The letter *y* is sometimes used as a vowel as well. The dictionary indicates how each vowel in each word is pronounced by using the following diacritical marks:

MACRON. The long straight mark over a vowel is called the **macron**. When the macron appears over a vowel, the vowel has the sound of its own name. Such vowels are called long vowels. The long vowel may mean the word has a silent *e* at the end. This can serve as a clue to help you spell the word.

    hate (hāt)   ride (rīd)
    meet (mēt)   low (lōw)

Note that the long ū sound is indicated in this pronunciation guide as yōo, *cute.*

BREVE. The vowels in the words *sat, red, fig, rod,* and *under* are called short vowels. In some dictionaries, the short vowels are left unmarked. In other dictionaries, the symbol called the **breve** (˘) is placed over short vowels.

>as (as) or (ăs)
>bed (bed) or (bĕd)
>lit (lit) or (lĭt)

CIRCUMFLEX. The vowel sounds in the words *all, horn,* and *law* are marked with the **circumflex** (ô).

>stall (stôl)　　shorn (shôrn)　　lawyer (lô · yər)

DIERESIS. The mark over the *a* in the words *ah, car,* and *partake* is called the **dieresis.**

>pälm　　scär　　pär·tak´

Consonant Sounds

All letters in the alphabet that are not vowels are consonants. Most consonants are pronounced in the same way in every word. One exception, however, is *c,* which may have a "hard" sound as in *came* or a "soft" sound as in *city.* The dictionary uses *k* to represent the "hard c" sound, and *s* to represent the "soft c."

>came (kām)　　cite (sīt)

EXERCISE 3: Put a macron or breve over the underlined vowels in the following words to show whether the vowel has a long or short pronunciation.

h<u>a</u>te	m<u>e</u>te	th<u>a</u>t
l<u>e</u>t	sp<u>i</u>t	c<u>e</u>de
r<u>o</u>te	m<u>u</u>st	h<u>a</u>s
b<u>u</u>n	l<u>i</u>ght	s<u>i</u>n
t<u>a</u>p	rep<u>e</u>l	d<u>e</u>tr<u>a</u>ct

EXERCISE 4: Rewrite each word using pronunciation symbols. Refer to the pronunciation guide on page 8.

bar	stone	height
sanity	peep	stale
polite	mute	pear
steppe	rot	straight
know	cord	excite
point	flower	book

Syllables

All dictionary entries of more than one syllable are divided into syllables. Each syllable is separated by a dot or dash.

pa·ja·mas (pə jam′əz, ·jä′məz) *n.pl.* [Hindi *pājāmā* < Per. *pāi*, a leg + *jāma*, garment] 1. in the Orient, a pair of loose silk or cotton trousers 2. a loosely fitting sleeping or lounging suit consisting of jacket (or blouse) and trousers —**pa·ja′ma** *adj.*

When you are not sure how a word should be spelled, try sounding it out by syllables. This can help you find the word in the dictionary. Is it *pur-haps* or *per-haps?* Check both spellings and you'll find the one you need. (It's *per-haps*.)

Knowing how a word is divided into syllables will also help when you must divide a word that does not fit on one line.

The diction-
ary is heavy.

Please pro-
nounce the word again.

EXERCISE 5: Draw a line between the syllables of the following words. Then look up each word in your dictionary to check your answers.

ingenious	disobedience	jurisprudence
fluorography	clandestine	munificent
disfavor	primeval	quarrelsome

Accent Mark

Find the word *palaver* in your dictionary and look at the pronunciation guide. In most dictionaries, there will be a dark slanted line over the second syllable. This is an accent mark. It tells you that the second syllable of *palaver* is accented or stressed. In some dictionaries the accent mark appears right after the stressed syllable; in others it appears right in front of it. (Note that some dictionaries have other ways of indicating stressed syllables.)

Some longer words have two accented syllables. That is, one syllable receives a heavier or primary stress and the other receives a lighter or secondary stress. The heavily accented syllable is marked with a heavy accent line; the lightly accented syllable is marked with a light accent line.

doc' · u · men' · ta · ry
ex · traor' · di · nar' · y

There's one more thing to know about accents: The accent in a word may shift from one syllable to another when the word is used as a different part of speech. For example:

fre' · quent (adjective)   re' · bound (noun)
fre · quent' (verb)   re · bound' (verb)

EXERCISE 6: **(a)** Mark the syllables and use pronunciation symbols to spell the following words.

psychology   psitticosis
photography   peasant
Polaroid   police

(b) Mark the primary accented syllables in the following words.

di·plo·ma·cy   me·di·ate   con·trol·ler
es·ca·late   me·dal·lion   ga·lac·tose
liq·ue·fac·tion   meat·ball   nom·i·na·tion

12 / Mastering Spelling

EXERCISE 7: In each sentence, copy the italicized words in the spaces provided. Mark the accented syllable and write *n* if the word is used as a noun, *v* if it is used as a verb, *a* if it is used as an adjective.

EXAMPLE: The *rebel* (re' bel *n*) was unable to *rebel* (re bel' *v*) any longer after he was sent to jail.

1. When will you *record* (_____) the Beatles' *record* (_____) for me?
2. Our schedule *projects* (_____) that all of these *projects* (_____) will reach completion in June.
3. The *contract* (_____) calls for metal parts that won't *contract* (_____) in cold weather.
4. When I *perfect* (_____) my new invention, consumers will be able to buy the world's first *perfect* (_____) mouse trap.

Part of Speech Labels

An abbreviation after each word in the dictionary tells what part of speech the word is.

car *n.* (noun)
bring *vt.* (transitive verb)
come *vi.* (intransitive verb)
beautiful *adj.* (adjective)
fully *adv.* (adverb)

of *prep.* (preposition)
and *conj.* (conjunction)
he *pron.* (pronoun)
hey *interj.* (interjection)

EXERCISE 8: For each word, write the abbreviation(s) for its part(s) of speech. Use your dictionary if you need help.

1. latent
2. wow
3. sleep
4. hardship
5. nor
6. radical
7. who
8. connive
9. they

10. smuggle	11. conquer	12. swiftly
13. hers	14. sing	15. for

Because many nouns can change to adjectives or verbs to nouns, the dictionary indicates when and how one part of speech changes to another. For example:

> ornament (noun)   to   ornamental (adjective)
> occur (verb)   to   occurrence (noun)

EXERCISE 9: Complete the following sentences by changing the word in parentheses to the part of speech indicated.

EXAMPLE: It took an hour to make the (install) <u>installation</u> (*n.*).

1. Won't someone please (promotion) _____(*v.*) my career as a rock star?
2. After my first hit record I plan to be a (reside) _____ (*n.*) in the most expensive apartment in town.
3. Despite the odds I am (hope) _____(*adj.*).
4. But just in case I fail, I plan (winner) _____(*v.*) the lottery.

Irregular Forms

Many nouns have irregular plurals. Many verbs have irregular past tense forms and irregular past participles. These irregular forms are listed in the dictionary. Thus, if you look up the noun *mouse,* you will find its plural, *mice.* Similarly, if you look up the verb *see,* you will find its past tense, *saw,* and its past participle, *seen.*

EXERCISE 10: (a) Use the dictionary to find the plural of the following nouns.

1. crocus		2. bellows
3. memorandum		4. life
5. axis		6. contralto

(b) Use the dictionary to find the past tense and past participle of the following verbs.

1. hang
2. catch
3. ride
4. sell
5. break
6. swim

Homonyms

Homonyms are words that have the same pronunciation but have different meanings and are usually spelled differently:

> **herd:** a group of animals
> **heard:** past tense of the verb *to hear*

Suppose you are looking up a word that is pronounced rēd. You want to find *reed*, a long-stemmed marsh grass, but you look under *read*. You will know from the definition that you have the wrong word and are probably dealing with a homonym. In that case, try another possible spelling. (For more about homonyms, see Chapter 9.)

EXERCISE 11: Write another word that has the same sound as each of the following.

boar	their	mane
here	steel	stair
hoarse	deer	lone

Other Confusing Sound-Alikes

You can often locate a word in the dictionary by sounding it out syllable by syllable and spelling it according to the way it sounds.

Indeed, most words are spelled as they sound. Think, for example, of *stamp, between,* and *bring.* Think of *consonant* and *vowel.* But what about *elephant,* which from the sound of it could be spelled *elefant?* What about *quiz,* which sounds as if it could be spelled *kwiz?* Or *television,* which sounds like *telavijun?*

It helps to remember that there is a pattern to many of the confusing letter-sound combinations. Often, for example, words contain a *ph* that sounds like *f,* and *qu* is almost always pronounced *kw (quiet, queen).* The *-sion* ending may be pronounced *jun* in some words *(decision)* and *shun* in others *(permission).* There are surely other patterns that are familiar to you.

Dictionary Skills / 15

But, as you probably already know, these are not the only confusing sounds in our language. Santa drives a *sleigh,* not a *slay.* And since the consonants *c, k,* and *ck* can all have the same pronunciation, how is anyone to know whether the timepiece on your desk is spelled *cloc, clok,* or *clock?*

The answer is that, until you know, you may have to look up more than one possible spelling.

We will look at more pronunciation problems in Chapter 8. In the meantime, have some fun figuring out the words whose pronunciations and meanings are given in the next exercise. Before you start, here's a hint: As you spell each word, remember that several letters in English words can be silent, or unpronounced. For example, if you ate out yesterday, you'll *k*now the restaurant had a si*g*n in front, you walked down an *a*isle to reac*h* your tabl*e,* and if you're feeling well ri*gh*t now you probably didn't get *p*tomai*n*e poisoning.

EXERCISE 12: Read the pronunciation and write the word. The meaning clue will help.

1. säm

   (a sacred song)

2. sī kō′ sis

   (a mental illness)

3. trôf

   (a food container for animals)

4. kwēnz

   (ruling females)

5. stäk

   (a share in a corporation)

6. laf

   (to express joy or amusement)

OTHER INFORMATION IN DICTIONARY ENTRIES

Definitions

Each word in the dictionary is defined. When a word has more than one meaning, each definition is numbered. Look for the definition that best fits your particular context.

pal·ate (pal′it) *n.* [ME. < L. *palatum*] **1.** the roof of the mouth, consisting of a hard bony forward part (the *hard palate*) and a soft fleshy back part (the *soft palate,* or *velum*) **2.** sense of taste: the palate was incorrectly thought to be the organ of taste **3.** intellectual taste; liking

PALATE

Synonyms and Antonyms

Synonyms are words with the same meaning:

>happy: joyful, joyous

Antonyms are words with the opposite meaning:

>happy: sad

Synonyms and/or antonyms are sometimes listed after the definition.

>**pale**¹ (pāl) *adj.* **pal'er, pal'est** [ME. < OFr. < L. *pallidus*, pale < *pallere*, to be pale < IE. base *pel-*, gray, pale, whence FALLOW²] **1.** of a whitish or colorless complexion; pallid; wan **2.** lacking intensity or brilliance: said of color, light, etc.; faint; dim **3.** feeble; weak *[a pale imitation]* —*vi.* **paled, pal'ing 1.** to become pale **2.** to seem weaker or less important —*vt.* to make pale —**pale'ly** *adv.* — **pale'ness** *n.*
>*SYN.*—**pale**, in this comparison the least connotative of these words, implies merely an unnatural whiteness or colorlessness, often temporary, of the complexion; **pallid** suggests a paleness resulting from exhaustion, faintness, emotional strain, etc.; **wan** suggests the paleness resulting from an emaciating illness; **ashen** implies the grayish paleness of the skin as in death; **livid** refers to a grayish-blue (now sometimes misunderstood as white or red) complexion, as of one in great rage or fear —*ANT.* **ruddy, rosy**

EXERCISE 13: (a) Write a synonym for each of the following words.

1. stay
2. murder
3. depressed
4. deceased
5. keep
6. mimic

(b) Write an antonym for the following words.

1. honest
2. shout
3. careful
4. most
5. probable
6. sell

Usage Labels

Usage labels characterize a word according to its appropriateness for a given purpose or situation. However, different dictionaries may assign differing usage labels to the same words. For example, the word *egghead* is labeled *slang* in one dictionary and not labeled as slang in another. While usage labels provide a good general guide, writers must eventually determine for themselves whether a word is appropriate for their context. *Webster's New World Dictionary* employs the usage labels that appear at the top of page 17.

Colloquial [Colloq.]: Characteristic of conversation and informal writing: *stuck up*

Slang: Coined terms and terms with new or extended meanings. They are not regarded as conventional or standard, but are used in very informal contexts: *bad* meaning good; *okay*

Archaic [Arch.] or Obsolete [Obs.]: Rarely used today except in certain restricted contexts such as religious ritual, but occurred in earlier writings: *yore,* formerly

Poetic [Poet.]: Used chiefly in poetry, especially in earlier poetry or in prose when poetic quality is desired: *o'er,* over

Dialect [Dial.]: Term used regularly in a particular geographic area: *y'all,* Southern for you

Foreign word(s): Words taken from other languages: *caveat emptor,* let the buyer beware (Latin)

EXERCISE 14: Use your dictionary to find the usage labels for the following words or word groups.

1. soul food
2. yon
3. jam session
4. sotto voce
5. vail
6. honcho

Etymology

Etymology refers to the origin and development or history of words. In the dictionary you will find that information in brackets following the part of speech label.

> **pal·a·tine**[1] (pal′ə tīn′, -tin) *adj.* [ME. < OFr. *palatin* < L. *palatinus* < *palatium*, PALACE] 1. of a palace 2. having royal privileges [a count *palatine*] 3. of or belonging to a count palatine or earl palatine 4. [P-] of the Palatinate —*n.* 1. an officer of an imperial palace 2. a medieval vassal lord having the rights of royalty in his own territory, or palatinate 3. a fur piece covering the shoulders 4. [P-] a native or inhabitant of the Palatinate —[P-] *see* SEVEN HILLS OF ROME

The following abbreviations are commonly used for the languages from which most English words have come:

Fr.	French	L.	Latin
OFr.	Old French	ME.	Middle English
G.	German	Mex.	Mexican
Gr.	Greek	OE.	Old English
Heb.	Hebrew	Sans.	Sanskrit
It.	Italian	Sp.	Spanish

18 / Mastering Spelling

Knowing the etymology of a word can sometimes help you remember how to spell that word. Etymology is especially useful in distinguishing between homonyms, those words that sound alike but are spelled differently. For example, let's see how etymology can help in the spelling of *right* and *write*. Both come from Old English words, spoken more than a thousand years ago. *Write* comes from *writan,* to scratch or engrave. *Right* comes from *riht,* straight or direct.

EXERCISE 15: Look up the following words and write the original language(s) and the word or words from which the present English word comes.

1. plastic
2. interfere
3. machine
4. idea
5. laud
6. municipal
7. reed
8. read
9. seed
10. cede

EXERCISES FOR REVIEW

A. Arrange the words in each group in alphabetical order by writing the numbers 1 to 5 above each word.

1. screwdrivers, pliers, hammers, wrenches, hacksaws
2. Mexico, Colombia, Argentina, Canada, Brazil
3. percale, perceive, perish, percolate, perdition
4. obvious, obey, obesity, object, oblige
5. impressive, impost, improper, improve, improvident
6. human, humane, huge, humble, humid
7. harmony, harpist, harvest, hatchet, harbor
9. adverbial, adverbs, allegory, agreement, apostrophe
10. pectic, pedestrian, pemmican, Penelope, pencil

B. Underline the words in each group which are located between the guide words.

parliamentarian
parlor
parody
parrot

parole
parish
parson

parry
parquet
parley
patriotic

seal
sea lamprey
sealant
sealed orders

sea scorpion
sea serpent
seamstress

search warrant
sear
search
sea king

Tennessee walking horse
tent
tentacle
tense

tennis
teosinte
tepee

teocalli
tenfold
Tennessee
tenor clef

emit
emitter
empennage
emolument

employ
employable
emission

emplane
emperor
empire
emplace

C. Use the pronunciation symbols on page 8 to write the pronunciations of the following words.

1. joust
2. manatee
3. parenthetical
4. liquescent
5. obsequious
6. quotidian
7. lissome
8. oligophagous
9. recalcitrant
10. bereave
11. benignant
12. hurdy gurdy

D. Using the pronunciation key, write the appropriate diacritical mark above the underlined vowels in the following words.

lathe
came
contact
bide
fun

train
redo
stick
shortening
cone

set
part
past
soil
room

E. Draw a vertical line between syllables and underline the accented syllables in each of the following words. Use your dictionary if necessary.

1. handsome
2. incidentally
3. athletics
4. perspiration
5. prejudice
6. dilapidated
7. fiasco
8. tournament
9. unanimous
10. Herculean
11. lucrative
12. irrelevant

F. For each italicized word, underline the accented syllable and write the part of speech. Use your dictionary if necessary.

1. I wish someone would *present* (_____) me with a *present* (_____).
2. Even if it were a *reject*, (_____) I wouldn't *reject* (_____) it.
3. Getting presents is a *subject* (_____) that does not *subject* (_____) me to any pain at all.
4. I'll always be a *rebel* (_____) and *rebel* (_____) against the saying, "It's better to give than to receive."

G. Write the part(s) of speech for each of the following words. Use your dictionary if necessary.

1. heckle
2. pedicab
3. countenance
4. marmot
5. scavenger
6. gloat
7. twice
8. intercede
9. emphatic
10. pensive
11. zowie
12. ouch
13. because
14. hardly
15. intermittent

H. Use your dictionary to find the past tense of the following verbs.

1. hear
2. say
3. stand
4. shut

5. cry
7. stick
9. lose

6. sting
8. bring
10. swim

11. run
13. wind
15. fly
17. kneel
19. hurt

12. write
14. get
16. freeze
18. lend
20. make

I. Use your dictionary to find the plurals of the following nouns.

1. child
3. goose
5. medium
7. foot
9. gas

2. deer
4. ox
6. thesis
8. tomato
10. ovum

11. wife
13. larva
15. dandy
17. hero
19. bus

12. spouse
14. fish
16. phenomenon
18. vertebra
20. piano

J. Write another word that sounds the same as each of the following.

1. neigh
4. meat
7. heart
10. so
13. pair

2. dear
5. weak
8. their
11. too
14. isle

3. here
6. forth
9. write
12. seen
15. bawl

22 / Mastering Spelling

K. The following words are misspelled. Use your dictionary to find the correct spelling.

1. vocifirous
2. mythilogical
3. vocabulery
4. metemorphasis
5. repelent
6. irrassible
7. pnumonia
8. irridescant
9. pachederm
10. equivicate
11. intermition
12. trembel
13. candedate
14. cinama
15. libary
16. complacate
17. restarant
18. sedintery
19. symtom
20. plesure

L. Write one synonym for each of the following words.

1. bestow
2. foyer
3. rescue
4. replace
5. disgrace
6. flash
7. huge
8. salary
9. choose
10. level

M. Write one antonym for each of the following words.

1. fault
2. friendly
3. pride
4. clouded
5. noise
6. keep
7. arrive
8. recent
9. sharp
10. scold

N. Look up each of the following words in your dictionary. What is the usage label?

1. vive
2. monkeyshine
3. aught
4. noddle
5. doth
6. cut dead
7. up-tight
8. fiver
9. flack
10. flivver
11. gyre
12. gyp
13. mayhap
14. pussyfoot
15. horsefeathers

O. Look up the following words and write the language(s) and the word or words from which the present English word comes.

1. gavel
2. gazette
3. float
4. domain
5. intercede
6. intelligence
7. larder
8. paean
9. monument
10. reckon
11. pajamas
12. goulash
13. chrome
14. course
15. goober
16. urban
17. Thursday
18. February
19. sauna
20. jog

3. SPELLING RULES

In this chapter you will study five basic rules of spelling. The rules will help you remember:

1. when to spell words with *ie* or *ei*
2. when to change *y* to *i* before a suffix*
3. when to drop a silent *e* before a suffix
4. when to double the final letter before a suffix
5. when to add a *k* after a final *c* before a suffix

The five rules are important because they tell you how to spell many common words. Practice exercises will help you understand and become familiar with the rules. Practice exercises will also help you recognize exceptions to the rules.

Use the pretest to find out which rules you need to work on and which you are already using because you know and understand them.

PRETEST

A. Fill in the blanks with *ei* or *ie*. If you have trouble with this section, plan to study "Rule One: ie/ei words" on pages 26 and 27.

1. bel____ve
2. l____sure
3. r____gn
4. rec____ve
5. dec____ve
6. h____ght
7. for____gner
8. pr____st
9. fr____nd
10. rec____pt
11. p____ce
12. misch____f

*A suffix is an ending such as *-ed, -ing, -ness,* or *-ship* that is added to a word to make a new word with a somewhat different meaning. For example:

stay + ed = stayed
float + ing = floating
dark + ness = darkness
friend + ship = friendship

Spelling Rules / 25

13. shr____k
14. pat____nt
15. handkerch____f
16. anc____nt
17. n____ce
18. ____ther

B. Add the indicated suffix and write the new word. If you have trouble with this section, plan to study "Rule Two: Words Ending in y" on pages 28 and 29.

1. dry + <u>ing</u>
2. day + <u>ly</u>
3. lovely + <u>ness</u>
4. sly + <u>ly</u>
5. apply + <u>ed</u>
6. accompany + <u>ing</u>
7. supply + <u>ing</u>
8. heavy + <u>est</u>
9. carry + <u>ing</u>
10. defy + <u>ed</u>
11. copy + <u>er</u>
12. easy + <u>est</u>
13. steady + <u>ness</u>
14. cry + <u>er</u>
15. shy + <u>ness</u>
16. shy + <u>ly</u>
17. lazy + <u>est</u>
18. enjoy + <u>ing</u>

C. Insert an e where necessary in the following blanks. If you have trouble with this section, plan to study "Rule Three: Words Ending in Silent e" on pages 31 through 33.

1. amus____ment
2. ach____ing
3. peac____ful
4. manag____able
5. outrag____ous
6. tru____ly
7. tast____ful
8. abridg____ing
9. su____ing
10. becom____ing
11. valu____able
12. wast____ing
13. mov____able
14. argu____ment
15. admir____able
16. excit____ing
17. requir____ment
18. hing____ing

D. Fill in the blanks where necessary. In some cases, you will need to double the consonant before adding the suffix. If you have trouble with this section, plan to study "Rule Four: The Doubling Rule" on pages 35, 36, and 39.

1. stun____ing
2. infer____ing
3. compel____ed
4. bat____er
5. occur____ence
6. refer____ing

26 / Mastering Spelling

7. drag____ed   8. control____able   9. prefer____ence
10. bag____age   11. cool____ing   12. allot____ing
13. drug____ist   14. war____ior   15. regret____ed
16. bid____er   17. blur____ed   18. depend____ence

E. Write a new word by adding the indicated suffix. Here's a hint: In some cases you will have to add the letter *k*. If you have trouble with this section, plan to study "Rule Five: Words Ending in *c*" on page 42.

1. picnic + <u>er</u>   2. frolic + <u>ing</u>
3. fantastic + <u>ally</u>   4. basic + <u>ally</u>
5. mimic + <u>ing</u>   6. shellac + <u>ed</u>
7. panic + <u>y</u>   8. republic + <u>an</u>
9. electric + <u>ity</u>   10. traffic + <u>ing</u>

RULE ONE: *IE/EI* WORDS

The following well-known rule on *ie/ei* words is so helpful that it's worth memorizing:

Place *i* before *e* except after *c*
Or when sounded as *a* in *neighbor* and *weigh*.

EXERCISE 1: Using the *ie/ei* rule as a guide, fill in the following blanks with *ie* or *ei*.

(a)

1. rec____ve   2. gr____f   3. p____ce
4. rel____ve   5. w____ght   6. rev____w
7. conc____ve   8. dec____t   9. perc____ve
10. y____ld   11. n____ce   12. s____ve
13. bel____ve   14. hyg____ne   15. c____ling
16. fr____ght.   17. fr____nd   18. ach____ve

(b)

1. v____n
2. ____ght
3. r____ndeer
4. shr____k
5. pr____st
6. f____nd
7. misch____f
8. p____r
9. dec____ve
10. v____l
11. sl____gh
12. r____gn
13. conc____t
14. rec____pt
15. th____ves
16. f____rce
17. sh____ld
18. ach____vement

Principal Exceptions to the *ie/ei* Rule

Here are two rules to help you remember the exceptions:

1. Words in the following nonsense sentence are spelled with *ei*:

    Neither leisured foreigner seized the weird height.

    However odd this sentence may sound to you, memorizing it will help you remember the exceptions.

2. When a word ends with the suffix *-ent*, put *i* before the *-ent* if the suffix is preceded by a *c* or *t* that has a soft (*sh*) sound.

    ancient   sufficient   quotient
    efficient   patient   proficient
         deficient

EXERCISE 2: Fill in the following blanks with *ei* or *ie*.

1. n____ther
2. conc____ve
3. ____ther
4. p____ce
5. h____ght
6. f____ld
7. effic____nt
8. for____gn
9. pat____nt
10. hyg____ne
11. fr____ght
12. w____ght
13. s____ze
14. l____sure
15. shr____k
16. defic____nt
17. rec____pt
18. suffic____nt

28 / Mastering Spelling

EXERCISE 3: Fill in the blanks with either *ei* or *ie*.

1. Have they rec____ved the package?
2. The f____ld work included digging at the site of an anc____nt village.
3. She sent a br____f note of thanks.
4. The doctor rev____wed the pat____nt's chart.
5. What is the h____ght from the floor to the c____ling?
6. He s____zed the baby and made him shr____k.
7. N____ther employee rec____ved a suffic____nt wage.
8. Our n____ghbor's cat was hurt in a f____rce fight with our dog.
9. My n____ce ach____ved a high mark on the test.
10. During our br____f visit to the zoo we saw several r____ndeer.
11. The ch____f reason he is overw____ght is that he overeats.
12. The th____ves were caught when the police perc____ved them.
13. The cashier was ineffic____nt so the rec____pts were defic____nt.
14. They couldn't bel____ve every p____ce of jewelry was gone.
15. In his l____sure time, the pr____st went to see his fr____nds.

EXERCISE 4: Correct the misspelled words.

1. sleigh
2. reindeer
3. releive
4. freinds
5. sheild
6. shreik
7. neither
8. siezed
9. reciept
10. seive
11. neice
12. eight

RULE TWO: WORDS ENDING IN *Y*

When a word ends in *y*, change the *y* to *i* before adding the suffixes *-ness* and *-ly*.

    steady + ly = steadily   sloppy + ly = sloppily
    steady + ness = steadiness   sloppy + ness = sloppiness

Note the exception to this rule: When a one-syllable adjective ends in *y* do NOT change the *y* to *i*.

dry + ly = dryly
dry + ness = dryness

shy + ly = shyly
shy + ness = shyness

When a word ends in *y* preceded by a consonant, change the *y* to *i* before a suffix that does not begin with an *i*.

lively + ness = liveliness
bury + al = burial

Exception:

bury + ing = burying

When a word ends in *y* preceded by a vowel, do NOT change the *y* to *i*.

enjoy + ed = enjoyed
played + ed = played

enjoy + ing = enjoying
play + ing = playing

Exceptions:

day—daily   lay—laid   pay—paid   say—said

EXERCISE 5: Write the *-ly* form of each of the following.

EXAMPLE: merry—merrily

1. ready
2. easy
3. angry
4. lucky
5. crazy
6. wry
7. spry
8. lazy
9. steady
10. necessary
11. day
12. clumsy
13. hasty
14. sly
15. hazy
16. heavy
17. hardy
18. weary

EXERCISE 6: Write the *-ed* form of each of the following.

EXAMPLE: rely—relied

1. busy
2. copy
3. obey
4. say
5. annoy
6. study

30 / Mastering Spelling

7. dry
8. deploy
9. defy
10. accompany
11. play
12. convey
13. destroy
14. spray
15. delay
16. apply
17. supply
18. imply

EXERCISE 7: Write the *-est* form of each of the following.
EXAMPLE: likely—likeliest

1. dry
2. happy
3. tasty
4. wavy
5. ugly
6. friendly
7. lonely
8. brainy
9. dizzy
10. lazy
11. sneaky
12. coy
13. weary
14. lovely
15. busy

EXERCISE 8: Write the *-er* form of each of the following.
EXAMPLE: sleepy—sleepier

1. happy
2. easy
3. rosy
4. merry
5. wealthy
6. likely
7. sticky
8. cozy
9. lucky
10. pretty
11. tardy
12. sturdy
13. heavy
14. busy
15. steady
16. rosy
17. fancy
18. lonely

EXERCISE 9: Write the *-ing* form of each of the following.
EXAMPLE: pray—praying

1. carry
2. glory
3. defy
4. pay
5. play
6. deny
7. vary
8. obey
9. imply
10. study
11. ready
12. supply

EXERCISE 10: Write the *-ness* form of each of the following.

EXAMPLE: sleepy—sleepiness

1. lovely
2. tasty
3. dizzy
4. sly
5. steady
6. crazy
7. lazy
8. icy
9. hardy
10. lonely
11. shy
12. hazy
13. dry
14. heavy
15. grumpy
16. ready
17. wry
18. sloppy

EXERCISE 11: Fill in the blanks with *y* or *i*.

1. Have they den____ed being there?
2. Phyllis left the room hast____ly.
3. His sense of humor has grown dr____er with the years.
4. They have destro____ed all the records.
5. Edna enjo____ed the performance.
6. She has been anno____ing me all morning with that question.
7. Your betra____al of our cause has upset our plans.
8. The abandoned puppy was in a pit____able state.
9. He wrote a play about lonel____ness.
10. I hope you're satisf____ed!
11. His glor____ous record will not be den____ed.
12. A stead____er hand than mine cop____ed that picture.
13. On his bus____est days, Phil pa____d us on time.
14. What are you impl____ing?
15. The ic____ness in his tone sa____d more than his words.

RULE THREE: WORDS ENDING IN SILENT *E*

When you add a suffix to a word ending in silent *e*, should you drop the silent *e*? The suffix will tell you.

32 / Mastering Spelling

1. Drop the silent *e* when you add suffixes beginning with a vowel (*-ing, -able, -ance, -ible, -or*):

   argue + ing = arguing
   love + able = lovable
   grieve + ance = grievance

   force + ible = forcible
   create + or = creator

2. Keep the silent *e* when you add suffixes beginning with a consonant (*-ment, -ty, -ful, -ly*):

   amuse + ment = amusement
   safe + ty = safety

   fate + ful = fateful
   fine + ly = finely

EXERCISE 12: Add the indicated suffix and write the new word.

EXAMPLES: take + <u>ing</u> = taking; fate + <u>ful</u> = fateful

1. tire + <u>ing</u>
2. rare + <u>ity</u>
3. date + <u>ing</u>
4. create + <u>or</u>
5. argue + <u>able</u>
6. fate + <u>ful</u>
7. recite + <u>al</u>
8. come + <u>ing</u>
9. lose + <u>ing</u>
10. receive + <u>able</u>

EXERCISE 13: Write the *-ment* form of each of the following.

EXAMPLE: agree—agreement

1. amuse
2. advise
3. place
4. arrange
5. manage
6. state
7. move
8. excite
9. atone

EXERCISE 14: Insert an *e* where necessary in the following blanks.

EXAMPLE: servic<u>e</u>able

(a)

1. reduc____ing
2. whol____ly
3. arriv____al
4. contriv____ance
5. nin____ty
6. encourag____ing

Spelling Rules / 33

7. confid____ing
8. wast____ful
9. smok____ing
10. ignor____ance
11. breez____y
12. peac____ful
13. desir____able
14. believ____able
15. advertis____ment

(b)

1. amus____ment
2. grac____ful
3. debat____ing
4. resourc____ful
5. ach____ing
6. stat____ment
7. resid____ing
8. tir____ing
9. reduc____ing
10. stat____ly
11. scarc____ly
12. us____able
13. outrac____ing
14. accurat____ly
15. recogniz____ing
16. debas____ment
17. pursu____ing
18. choos____ing

Principal Exceptions to the Silent e Rule

1. When words end in *ie*, drop the silent *e* and change the *i* to *y* before adding *-ing*.

       lie—lying   tie—tying   belie—belying

2. To prevent confusion with other words that are similar, *dye* and *singe* retain the *e* before adding *-ing*.

   dye (to color) becomes *dyeing* (NOT *dying*, which means to expire). *singe* (to scorch) becomes *singeing* (NOT *singing*, which means to produce music vocally).

3. Drop the silent *e* in *truly, duly, argument, bluish, ninth*.
4. Keep the silent *e* in *canoeing, shoeing, hoeing*.
5. When words end in *ce* and *ge*, keep the silent *e* before adding suffixes starting with a vowel (such as *-able* and *-ous*) to preserve the soft sound of *c* and *g*.

   notice—noticing *but* noticeable
   courage—encouraging *but* courageous

   NOTE: When words end in *dge* the preferred form omits the *e* (*judgment*); however, keeping the *e* is acceptable (*judgement*).

34 Mastering Spelling

EXERCISE 15: Add the indicated suffix and write the new word.

EXAMPLE: write + <u>ing</u> = writing

1. persuade + <u>ing</u>
2. judge + <u>ment</u>
3. lie + <u>ing</u>
4. prove + <u>able</u>
5. die + <u>ing</u>
6. sue + <u>ing</u>
7. dye + <u>ing</u>
8. advantage + <u>ous</u>
9. courage + <u>ous</u>
10. place + <u>ment</u>
11. manage + <u>ing</u>
12. arrange + <u>ment</u>
13. manage + <u>able</u>
14. love + <u>able</u>
15. nine + <u>th</u>
16. lodge + <u>ing</u>
17. taste + <u>ful</u>
18. state + <u>ment</u>
19. practice + <u>ing</u>
20. outrage + <u>ous</u>
21. true + <u>ly</u>
22. argue + <u>ing</u>
23. service + <u>able</u>
24. service + <u>ing</u>

EXERCISE 16: Write the *-able* form of each of the following.

EXAMPLE: advise—advisable

1. like
2. agree
3. insure
4. manage
5. excite
6. conceive
7. value
8. retrace
9. argue
10. move
11. receive
12. sale
13. admire
14. use
15. size
16. pleasure
17. compare
18. confine

EXERCISE 17: Insert an *e* where necessary in the following blanks.

1. The men have been argu____ing all day.
2. We were convinc____ed by the evidence.
3. It was surpris____ing to learn how resource____ful you are.
4. His argu____ment ended when the judge arrived.

5. If his car is servic____able, the manag____ment will trade it in.
6. Fleec____y clouds are rac____ing over the treetops.
7. The preced____ing summary was pleas____ingly presented.
8. Jerry has been blam____ing us without recogniz____ing his own problem.
9. Cano____ing through the rapids requires a courag____ous attitude.
10. Ignit____ing the flare, the rescuers stopped their fatigu____ing work.
11. The plac____ment bureau has been promis____ing me a suitable position for weeks.
12. In my judg____ment, he is rar____ly here.
13. Desir____ing a better salary, she is pursu____ing a new career.
14. Ignor____ance is a poor excuse.
15. The nin____th contestant receiv____ed some blu____ish-ting____ed flowers.

EXERCISE 18: Correct the misspelled words.

1. placment
2. serviceing
3. housing
4. noticeing
5. changing
6. rageing
7. lieing
8. improvement
9. unnoticeable
10. surpriseingly
11. moveable
12. movment

RULE FOUR: THE DOUBLING RULE

Often, when a word ends in a consonant, the consonant is doubled before a suffix is added to it. How do you know when this doubled consonant must appear? Why is there a doubled consonant in prefe<u>rr</u>-ed but a single consonant in prefe<u>r</u>-ence? The Doubling Rule will help you recognize what condition must be met before you can proceed to double a final consonant.

For convenience we will apply the Doubling Rule to words of one syllable before we apply it to words of more than one syllable.

One-Syllable Words and the Doubling Rule

Words of one syllable are words that contain a single vowel sound. When a suffix is added to a one-syllable word, double the final consonant of the word *only if both of the following conditions are true:*

1. the suffix begins with a vowel (*-ing, -ed, -er, -est, -y,* for example)

    and

2. the word ends in a single consonant preceded by a single vowel (vowel + consonant combination, or **vc**)

$$\begin{array}{ccc} \text{vc} & \text{vc} & \text{vc} \\ \text{tan—tanning} & \text{wrap—wrapped} & \text{wit—witty} \end{array}$$

DO NOT DOUBLE the final consonant if the suffix begins with a consonant (*-ment, -less, -ness, -ly,* for example):

$$\begin{array}{c} \text{v} \quad \text{c} \\ \text{fit—fitted } but\ not\ \text{fitness} \end{array}$$

DO NOT DOUBLE the final consonant when the word ends in two consonants (consonant + consonant combination, or **cc**) *or* in a final consonant preceded by two vowels (vowel + vowel + consonant combination, or **vvc**):

$$\begin{array}{cc} \text{cc} \quad \text{cc} & \text{vvc} \quad \text{vvc} \\ \text{want—wanted} & \text{boil—boiling} \end{array}$$

EXERCISE 19: Add the indicated suffix and write the new word.

1. stop + <u>ed</u>
2. quaint + <u>ly</u>
3. hot + <u>est</u>
4. send + <u>ing</u>
5. cup + <u>ful</u>
6. sing + <u>ing</u>
7. steam + <u>ing</u>
8. dark + <u>ly</u>
9. win + <u>some</u>
10. tour + <u>ing</u>
11. slope + <u>ing</u>
12. stamp + <u>ed</u>
13. time + <u>ed</u>
14. stun + <u>ed</u>
15. clap + <u>ing</u>

EXERCISE 20: Fill in the blanks where necessary. In some cases you will have to double the final consonant before adding the suffix.

1. The children were hop____ing the rabbit would start hop____ing.
2. Who tap____ed the music for you?

3. She turned when he tap____ed her on the shoulder.
4. The carpenter plan____ed the wood to give it a smooth surface.
5. Ken plan____ed to go to Greece on vacation.
6. In some cultures star____ing at someone is not considered rude.
7. My friend was given the star____ing role in the new show.
8. The dog's hair was tangled and mat____ed.
9. Spring is the mat____ing season for many species.
10. The hairdresser's smallest scissors are called snip____ers.
11. The neighborhood was terrified until the snip____er was caught.
12. Grandparents often dote on their grandchildren, but dot____ing can turn into spoiling.
13. That artist has a distinctive way of dot____ing his i's and crossing his t's.
14. All workers occasionally gripe about their jobs, but constant grip____ing is irritating to the rest of the staff.
15. One way to open a bottle of wine is by grip____ing the cork and turning the bottle.

EXERCISE 21: Write the -er form of each of the following. Note: Adding -er to a noun makes it a person who does something.

EXAMPLE: wrap—wrapper

Adding -er to an adjective makes it the comparative form of that adjective.

EXAMPLE: dim—dimmer

1. bat	2. damp	3. blot
4. prim	5. wet	6. swim
7. drum	8. find	9. kind
10. lend	11. hard	12. limp
13. sin	14. slim	15. load
16. hit	17. proud	18. rob

38 / Mastering Spelling

EXERCISE 22: Write the *-ing* form of each of the following in the space provided.

EXAMPLE: drop—dropping

1. beg	2. rub	3. bet
4. run	5. scrub	6. coat
7. stop	8. fly	9. act
10. spend	11. blur	12. stamp
13. boat	14. ship	15. cap
16. let	17. war	18. star

EXERCISE 23: Write the *-ed* form of each of the following.

EXAMPLE: tap—tapped

1. rub	2. soil	3. sand
4. fix	5. ban	6. pour
7. slit	8. slip	9. clip
10. flip	11. blur	12. drug
13. drill	14. fan	15. add
16. pack	17. train	18. drop

EXERCISE 24: Add the indicated suffix and write the new word.

EXAMPLE: plot + ing = plotting

1. wed + ed	2. blur + y
3. beg + ar	4. drug + ist
5. rob + ery	6. ship + er
7. wit + less	8. skin + y
9. act + ion	10. war + ior
11. gas + ed	12. turn + ing
13. wit + y	14. wet + ness

15. bid + <u>er</u>
16. stop + <u>age</u>
17. pool + <u>ing</u>
18. poll + <u>ing</u>

Words of More than One Syllable and the Doubling Rule

The Doubling Rule is applied to words of more than one syllable *only* when the word with the suffix added is pronounced with the accent on the syllable preceding the suffix. Thus, if a word has two or more syllables and the last syllable of the word will be accented or stressed when the suffix is added, then the Doubling Rule is used.

    measure + ing   accent not on last syllable   measuring
    metal + ic   accent will be on last syllable   metal'lic

NOTE: When a suffix is added there can be changes in the syllable that gets stressed:

        me'tal   metal'lic

Remember that, according to the Doubling Rule, the final consonant is doubled *only if* the word ends in a single consonant preceded by a single vowel (**vc** combination) *and* the suffix begins with a vowel.

defer + ed = deferred   because stress is on final syllable before suffix *and* suffix starts with a vowel *and* word ends with **vc**

BUT

defer + ment = deferment   because suffix begins with consonant

defer + ence = deference   because stress moves to first syllable

begin + er = beginner   repel + ant = repellant

BUT

contain + er = container   repent + ing = repenting

EXERCISE 25:   Add the indicated suffix and write the new word.

1. submit + <u>ed</u>
2. except + <u>ing</u>
3. prefer + <u>ed</u>
4. model + <u>ed</u>

5. merit + ed
6. cancel + ed
7. prefer + ence
8. contain + ed
9. unfit + ing
10. deter + ed

EXERCISE 26: Write the -ed form of the following.

1. admit
2. conquer
3. occur
4. regret
5. confer
6. dislike
7. excel
8. control
9. extol
10. propel
11. submit
12. brighten
13. compel
14. offer
15. diet
16. transmit
17. better
18. impair

EXERCISE 27: Add the indicated suffix and write the new word.

1. retreat + ed
2. transfer + ence
3. admit + ance
4. infer + ed
5. transfer + ed
6. differ + ence
7. utter + ance
8. occur + ence
9. conceal + ing
10. rebel + ion
11. defer + ence
12. prefer + ed
13. defer + ed
14. prefer + ence
15. reside + ence
16. equip + ing
17. allot + ed
18. control + able

EXERCISE 28: Add the indicated suffix and write the new word.

1. ship + ing
2. skip + ed
3. hot + est
4. transfer + ing
5. exploit + ed
6. alter + able
7. regard + less
8. wit + y

9. plot + ing
10. infer + ence
11. confer + ence
12. drag + ing
13. entail + ed
14. admit + ing
15. occur + ence
16. occur + ed

EXERCISE 29: Fill in the blank where you need to double the final consonant.

1. It was the wit____iest remark of the evening.
2. The porcelain figure was carefully wrap____ed.
3. Oliver beg____ed for another bowl of ice cream.
4. The crew repel____ed the enemy attempt to board the vessel.
5. Stop____ing at nothing, they plot____ed to overthrow the government.
6. The wet____est part of the slip____ery deck was roped off.
7. He readily admit____ed his vision was blur____ed.
8. His refer____ence to our meeting impel____ed us to tell the facts.
9. Are you commit____ed to uncontrol____ed spending?
10. He defer____ed his departure until tomorrow.
11. It occur____ed to me we might not solve this knot____y problem.
12. We were forbid____en to enter the room while the enamel____er was at work.
13. It is regret____able your confer____ence was postponed.
14. Since the allot____ed time has expired, the contract is annul____ed.

EXERCISE 30: Circle the misspelled word in each group and write it correctly.

1. tagging   submited   knitter
2. regrettable   transmision   runner
3. winning   prefered   batted
4. recuring   detaining   spinner

5. piloted	claimant	compeled
6. profitted	clamming	interacted
7. streaming	stalking	occurence
8. blessed	corresponded	alloting
9. swiming	jogging	planted

RULE FIVE: WORDS ENDING IN C

Many words such as *picnic* and *panic* end in a hard *c* sound. To keep that hard *c* sound when adding a suffix beginning with *e*, *i*, or *y*, insert *k* before the suffix.

    picnic—picnicking   panic—panicking

EXERCISE 31: Add the indicated suffix and write the new word.

1. picnic + er
2. republic + an
3. drastic + ally
4. dramatic + ally
5. energetic + ally
6. colic + y
7. shellac + ing
8. traffic + ing
9. frantic + ally
10. critic + ally
11. ecstatic + ally
12. mystic + al
13. frolic + ing
14. basic + ally
15. mimic + ing
16. lyric + al
17. fantastic + ally
18. panic + ed

EXERCISE 32: Fill in the blanks with *k* where necessary.

1. The senator public____ly announced her candidacy.
2. He threw the frisbee energetic____ally.
3. The picnic____ers went home when the rain started.
4. The newly shellac____ed floors were shining.

5. Everyone on the team had a physic____al examination.
6. The panic____y parents called the police.
7. Joan's facelift changed her appearance dramatic____ally.
8. Basic____ally, I agree with you.
9. Is it time for your annual physic____al?
10. The baby was colic____y last month.

EXERCISES FOR REVIEW

A. Fill in the following blanks with *ei* or *ie*.

1. great rel____f
2. p____ce of paper
3. sl____gh bells
4. heavyw____ght boxer
5. high c____ling
6. rent rec____pt
7. ____ght reasons
8. n____ther of them
9. tight r____ns
10. fr____ndly student
11. s____ze the hour
12. suffic____nt reason
13. effic____nt help
14. l____sure time
15. w____rd noise
16. defic____nt in math
17. misch____vous child
18. pat____nt teacher
19. f____ld day
20. kind for____gner

B. Add the indicated suffix and write the new word.

1. weary + <u>ly</u>
2. pry + <u>ing</u>
3. tasty + <u>est</u>
4. risky + <u>est</u>
5. obey + <u>ed</u>
6. carry + <u>ing</u>
7. friendly + <u>est</u>
8. busy + <u>er</u>
9. likely + <u>er</u>
10. deny + <u>al</u>
11. steady + <u>ing</u>
12. cry + <u>er</u>
13. unmercy + <u>fully</u>
14. dry + <u>ly</u>

44 / Mastering Spelling

15. say + ed
16. brainy + est
17. imply + ing
18. lucky + ly
19. shy + ness
20. apply + ing

C. Insert an e where necessary in the following blanks.

1. valu____able gem
2. outrag____ous plan
3. bank stat____ment
4. reduc____ing diet
5. dy____ing black
6. sho____ing a horse
7. prov____able
8. courag____ous fighter
9. notic____able error
10. insur____ing peace
11. hour of excit____ment
12. manag____able plan
13. servic____able
14. cas____ment window
15. choos____ing officers
16. neat arrang____ment
17. logical argu____ment
18. new abridg____ment
19. du____ly noted
20. sing____ing the hair

D. Fill in the blanks where necessary. In some cases you will need to double the final consonant before adding the suffix.

1. hot____est day
2. blot____ed out
3. rub____ing alcohol
4. rot____ed stump
5. metal____ic surface
6. prefer____ed position
7. slip____ed up
8. well equip____ed
9. drag____ed out
10. clear refer____ence
11. plan____ed program
12. din____ing room
13. bat____er up
14. commit____ee room
15. submit____ed bill
16. prefer____ence shown
17. stand____ing still
18. impel____ing necessity
19. coat____ed candy
20. offer____ing security

E. Fill in the blanks where necessary. In some cases you will need to double the final consonant before adding the suffix.

1. It was a most unpleasant occur____ence.
2. Have you transmit____ed our offer to their firm?
3. Hail the conquer____ing hero!
4. We ate lunch at the confer____ence table.
5. The president regret____ed the incident.
6. The family defer____ed to her wishes.
7. Her mother extol____ed her virtues.
8. He is commit____ed to the program.
9. He made an amazing infer____ence.
10. Why do you think swim____ing is so popular?

F. Insert the missing letter where necessary.

1. mystic____al memories
2. mimic____ed his elders
3. former Republic____an
4. critic____al analysis
5. frolic____ed gaily
6. shellac____ing the floor
7. electric____al energy
8. tired picnic____ers
9. lyric____al outburst
10. panic____y participants

4. FORMING PLURALS

Plurals of nouns are generally formed in predictable ways. Most plurals follow one of several basic rules. In this chapter we will review those rules and examine some interesting exceptions to them. In this chapter you will learn how to spell the plural forms of:

1. nouns to which *s* or *es* are added
2. nouns which change when their final letter is *f* or *y*
3. words that do not change
4. words that change internally
5. compound nouns and foreign words
6. signs, numbers, and words being used as words

First, take the following pretest to determine what problems you have, if any, in spelling plural forms. The rules and exercises that follow will strengthen your ability in the areas in which you need practice.

PRETEST

A. Write the plural form of each of the following words. If you have trouble with this section, plan to study Rules 1 through 4 for forming regular plurals on pages 47 and 48.

newspaper	studio	waltz
cello	clutch	flame
emblem	scenario	clod
tax	brass	embargo

B. Write the plural form of each of the following words. If you have trouble with this section, plan to study Rules 5 through 7 for forming regular plurals on pages 48 and 49.

Forming Plurals / 47

ally	comedy	monkey
tray	chief	elf
life	knife	wharf
valley	bluff	proof

C. Write the plural form of each of the following words. If you have trouble with this section, plan to study Rule 8 for forming irregular plurals on page 51.

sheep	man	ox
wheat	traffic	dozen
fish	deer	mouse
goose	child	woman

D. Write the plural form of each of the following words. If you have trouble with this section, plan to study Rule 9 for forming the plural of foreign words on pages 52 and 53.

bacterium	madame	focus
spectrum	alga	hypothesis
phenomenon	crisis	trousseau
alumnus	vertebra	basis

E. Write the plural form of each of the following words. If you have trouble with this section, plan to study Rules 10 and 11 on pages 54 and 55.

but	son-in-law	7
glassful	t	hanger-on
son-of-a-gun	teaspoonful	editor-in-chief
breakthrough	major general	lily-of-the-valley

RULES FOR FORMING REGULAR PLURALS

RULE 1: Add *s* to the singular noun form.

        magazine—magazines   train—trains

48 / Mastering Spelling

RULE 2: Add *es* to the singular noun when it ends in *s, x, z, ch,* and *sh*. A good way to remember this rule is to add *es* if the plural has an extra syllable when you pronounce it.

    glass—glasses   ax—axes
    waltz—waltzes   witch—witches

RULE 3: Add *s* to nouns ending in *o* preceded by a vowel.

    patio—patios   radio—radios

RULE 4: Add *es* to nouns ending in *o* preceded by a consonant.

    cargo—cargoes   hero—heroes

EXCEPTIONS: Some words which end in *o* preceded by a consonant are exceptions to this rule. The following words form their plurals by adding *s*:

altos	kimonos	sopranos
autos	pianos	stilettos
broncos	silos	tobaccos
Eskimos	solos	torsos
Filipinos	sombreros	tacos

EXERCISE 1: Write the plural form of each of the following.

1. picnic   2. guess   3. torso
4. view   5. march   6. surplus
7. branch   8. science   9. studio
10. folio   11. hero   12. time
13. glass   14. rich   15. phlox
16. Eskimo 17. rodeo   18. trap

RULE 5: Add *s* to nouns ending in *y* when the *y* is preceded by a vowel

  day—days   alley—alleys   valley—valleys

RULE 6: When a word ends in *y* preceded by a consonant, change the *y* to *i* and add *es*, except in proper names when *s* is added.

    fly—flies   ally—allies
    Mary—Marys   Nancy—Nancys

EXERCISE 2: Change each of the following to its plural form.

1. supply
2. attorney
3. property
4. Amy
5. lily
6. turkey
7. Friday
8. city
9. cemetery
10. enemy
11. quality
12. quantity

RULE 7: Nouns ending in *f* and *fe*: There is no general rule governing which words form the plural by adding *s* and which words change the *f* and *fe* to *v* and add *es*. However, if the *f* (or *fe*) is preceded by a long vowel or by *l*, you can usually change the *f* (or *fe*) to *v* and add *es*.

    calf—calves   half—halves   life—lives
    elf—elves   knife—knives   thief—thieves
    self—selves   leaf—leaves   wife—wives
    sheaf—sheaves   loaf—loaves   wolf—wolves

The following plurals are exceptions to the *f* rule:

    briefs   cliffs   bluffs   wharfs or wharves
    proofs   roofs   chiefs   hoofs or hooves
    chefs   cuffs   giraffes   dwarfs or dwarves
    beliefs*   griefs*   reefs   scarfs or scarves
    turfs

   *Note that the plural of *belief* is *beliefs*. If you change the *f* to *v* and add *es*, you have the word *believes*. This word has a different meaning and is a different part of speech.

    A body of religious *beliefs* is called a creed. (*beliefs* is a noun)
    Dan *believes* he is the best man on the team. (*believes* is a verb)

   Similarly, the plural of *grief* is *griefs*. *Grieves* is a verb.

EXERCISE 3: Write the plural forms of each of the following.

(a)

1. werewolf
2. jackknife
3. half
4. hoof
5. yourself
6. puff
7. chief
8. roof
9. midwife
10. giraffe

(b)

Complete the following sentences with the correct form of the word in parentheses.

1. (beliefs/believes) According to my friend's _____, I need to study these spelling rules.
2. (loafs/loaves) While I was studying last night, he baked two _____ of bread.
3. (proofs/proves) Hey, how many _____ do you need that I know these words!
4. (griefs/grieves) In fact, studying this lesson has caused me more _____ than I can count.

EXERCISE 4: Write the plural form of each of the following nouns.

1. strawberry
2. portfolio
3. lady
4. ladybug
5. dozen
6. knife
7. roof
8. ghost
9. hoax
10. radio
11. birch
12. fox
13. taco
14. alley
15. Michael
16. ally
17. Sunday
18. entity
19. boundary
20. shelf

RULES FOR FORMING IRREGULAR PLURALS

RULE 8: A few English nouns do not change when the plural is formed. That is, their singular and plural forms are the same.

corps	wheat	trout
deer	barley	mackerel
grouse	rye	**gross**
series	traffic	**dozen**
sheep	buffalo	**fish**

NOTE: This rule applies when you refer to more than one thing, animal, etc.

> We caught ten trout.
> Six deer crossed the road.

However, when you mean species or varieties of animals, grains, or fish, use a standard plural.

> Many wheats are grown throughout the world.
> There are different kinds of basses in American waters.

The plural of some words is formed by an internal spelling change. Others add an ending other than *s*. Among the most common of these are:

ox—oxen	die—dice	child—children
foot—feet	man—men	woman—women
goose—geese	mouse—mice	tooth—teeth

BUT: mongooses (not mongeese!) from the Indian word *mangūs*.

EXERCISE 5: Write the plural forms of the following nouns.

1. tooth
2. sheep
3. child
4. gentleman
5. shrimp
6. sunfish
7. series
8. gross
9. ox
10. mouse
11. goose
12. wheat

52 / Mastering Spelling

RULE 9: Foreign words

Some foreign words that have entered our vocabulary keep the plural form of their original language instead of adding the English *s* or *es*. You are most likely to find many of these words when you read scientific, technical, or academic material. However, some are in everyday use. Most of these words are of Latin or French origin. Familiarize yourself with the words listed below that you are most likely to need.

addendum—addenda
alumna (female)—alumnae
antenna—antennae
axis—axes
bacterium—bacteria
beau—beaux
chapeau—chapeaux
crisis—crises
datum—data
erratum—errata
fungus—fungi
hypothesis—hypotheses
madame—mesdames
minutia—minutiae
nebula—nebulae
oasis—oases
phenomenon—phenomena
spectrum—spectra
synopsis—synopses
thesis—theses
vertebra—vertebrae

alga—algae
alumnus (male)—alumni
antithesis—antitheses
bacillus—bacilli
basis—bases
candelabrum—candelabra
cortex—cortices
curriculum—curricula
ellipsis—ellipses
focus—foci
genus—genera
larva—larvae
medium—media
monsieur—messieurs
nucleus—nuclei
parenthesis—parentheses
radius—radii
stimulus—stimuli
synthesis—syntheses
trousseau—trousseaux

NOTE: The word *media* is the plural of *medium*. *Media* is often used when referring to radio, television, newspapers, and movies. Since it is a plural word, it is correct to use it when speaking of more than one method of communication. However, when you refer to radio alone, or television alone, it is correct to use the word *medium*. For example:

Newspapers are a print *medium*.

For some words both an English plural and a plural in the original language are acceptable. Often the English plural is preferred, as shown in the list of words at the top of page 53.

index—indexes or indices
appendix—appendixes or appendices
formula—formulas or formulae
memorandum—memorandums or memoranda
cello—cellos or celli
contralto—contraltos or contralti

In such cases the first plural form given in the dictionary is preferred, but the second is also correct.

EXERCISE 6: Complete the following sentences with the correct form of the word in parentheses.

1. (beau/beaux) My sister likes to call our boyfriends _____.
2. (alumnus/alumni) Two of them are _____ of a college in New York.
3. (crisis/crises) Bob is still studying hard and always seems to be in a state of _____.
4. (thesis/theses) When Jenny and Mike finish writing their _____, we'll all be happier.
5. (parenthesis/parentheses) Please put the following in _____.
6. (chapeau/chapeaux) All my cousin's _____ are awful!
7. (antithesis/antitheses) Her taste is the _____ of mine.
8. (cortex/cortices) It's obvious our _____ have not developed in the same way.
9. (trousseau/trousseaux) Why is she convinced she has the best-looking clothes in both our _____ ?

EXERCISE 7: Write the singular form of the following words.

1. alumnae
2. syntheses
3. phenomena
4. data

5. mesdames
7. curricula
9. nuclei
11. beaux
6. foci
8. bases
10. cortices
12. genera

RULE 10: Forming the plurals of letters, numbers, signs, and acronyms

When forming the plural of numbers, signs, acronyms, and other unusual characters used as nouns, add *s* if the resulting form will not be confusing.

> The 1920s are the years of the Lost Generation.
> There are many YWCAs in Chicago.
> Writing IOUs by the dozen, he plunged more deeply into debt.
> When I am in a hurry, my papers are filled with %s and &s.

But when forming the plurals of letters, and in any case where the resulting form would be confusing if *s* alone were added, the plural is formed by adding an apostrophe and an *s*.

> In that school the 8's and 9's are always getting into trouble.
> She was so old-fashioned that she kept minding her p's and q's.
> The Coast Guard reported numerous SOS's on the day of the hurricane.
> Don't give me any if's, and's, or but's.

EXERCISE 8: Write the plural forms of the following.

1. and
2. &
3. 10
4. m
5. z
6. %
7. R
8. 1980
9. !

EXERCISE 9: Write the plural forms of the following irregular words.

1. deer
2. alumna
3. radius
4. wheat
5. sunfish
6. foot
7. mouse
8. child
9. series
10. genus

11. woman
12. k
13. and
14. goose
15. ox
16. #
17. 16
18. sheep
19. monsieur
20. oasis
21. spectrum
22. corn
23. crisis
24. beau

FORMING PLURALS OF COMPOUND WORDS

RULE 11: The plurals of compounds words can be formed in two ways:

A. If the compound noun is a solid word, the *s* is placed at the end:

    armful—armfuls   breakthrough—breakthroughs

B. If the compound noun is hyphenated or is composed of two words, add *s* to the noun, not to the modifier.

    editor-in-chief—editors-in-chief
    son-in-law—sons-in-law

In these examples the words *in-chief* and *in-law* modify the nouns *editor* and *son*. Therefore, the nouns are changed to their plural forms. In other words, the most important element in the compound word is changed to the plural form.

What is the correct plural of *major general?* Of *postmaster general?* In these two-word compounds, the word "general" is used in two different ways. The plurals are, respectively, *major generals* and *postmasters general*. This is because, in the compound *major general*, *major* is an adjective modifying *general*. But in the other example, *general* is used as an adjective, in an unusual position for English, to modify *postmaster*. The *postmaster general* is the chief postmaster, or the postmaster who supervises all the other postmasters. This title form is used primarily for the heads of Federal government agencies. Thus we have the *attorney general*, who heads the Department of Justice. There may be a succession of *attorneys general* during a President's administration.

EXERCISE 10: Write the plural forms of the following words.

1. daughter-in-law
2. stepbrother
3. vice admiral
4. shipbuilder
5. commander-in-chief
6. councilmember
7. chairperson
8. teaspoonful
9. go-between
10. looker-on
11. houseful
12. standby
13. surgeon general
14. sergeant-at-arms
15. lily-of-the-valley
16. lieutenant colonel
17. cupful
18. gentleman

EXERCISES FOR REVIEW

A. Change each of the following to its plural form.

1. catch
2. quantity
3. guess
4. bus
5. rodeo
6. tomato
7. company
8. auto
9. kimono
10. alley
11. Monday
12. comedy
13. Harry
14. Filipino
15. valley
16. picnic
17. jockey
18. donkey
19. attorney
20. soprano
21. flash
22. papa
23. ally
24. hoax

B. Change each of the following to its plural form.

1. wife
2. staff
3. survey
4. try
5. jury
6. lobby
7. porch
8. puff
9. fife
10. echo
11. calf
12. belief

Forming Plurals / 57

13. holiday
14. tornado
15. money
16. chief
17. identity
18. scarf
19. wax
20. latch
21. berry
22. alto
23. turkey
24. thief

C. Write the singular form of each of the following words.

1. knives
2. cavities
3. torsos
4. loaves
5. monies
6. Sallys
7. riches
8. pantries
9. donkeys
10. chefs
11. bluffs
12. masses
13. wolves
14. boxes
15. roofs
16. summaries
17. hooves
18. companies

D. Write the plural form of each of these words.

1. baby
2. story
3. valley
4. glitch
5. beast
6. piano
7. daddy
8. gulf
9. solo
10. duty
11. elf
12. lady
13. load
14. folio
15. buffalo
16. city
17. army
18. journey
19. tomato
20. plane
21. fairy

E. Preceding each sentence there are two or three singular nouns. Fill the blanks in the sentences with the correct plural forms in the given order.

1. (purchase/tea/avocado) Among the _____ were _____ and _____.
2. (hero/radio) Many of the disabled _____ did not have field _____.

58 / Mastering Spelling

3. (leaf/cliff) The _____ of the trees along the _____ were falling.
4. (horse/cattle) We saw many _____ and _____ in the valley.

F. In each blank write the plural of the word which follows in parentheses.

1. In many _____ (place) _____ (sheep) are raised.
2. At the _____ (party) many _____ (dish) were used.
3. The _____ (man) and the _____ (child) were boating in the park.
4. The _____ (chimpanzee) migrated into the _____ (valley).
5. The _____ (woman) sold two bushels of _____ (potato).
6. The _____ (box) were sent to many different _____ (city).
7. The _____ (goose) were kept in a pen which was twenty _____ (foot) long.
8. We saw several _____ deer and _____ (ox) in the field.

G. Change each of the following words to its plural form.

1. moose
2. nucleus
3. larva
4. synthesis
5. trout
6. candelabrum
7. ox
8. monsieur
9. louse
10. goose
11. grandchild
12. Congresswoman
13. series
14. foreman
15. spectrum

16. 14	17. corn	18. shrimp
19. %	10. s	21. COD
22. traffic	23. corps	24. catfish

H. Change each of the following words to its plural form.

1. chief executive officer
2. mother-in-law
3. pocketful
4. hanger-on
5. half brother
6. stepbrother
7. lieutenant colonel
8. attorney general
9. tablespoonful
10. tabletop
11. vice president
12. ghost writer

I. Write the plural form of each word in parentheses.

1. The (berry) _____ are especially tasty after the rain.
2. Take two (spoonful) _____ every three hours.
3. The (reef) _____ have always been a haven for (castaway) _____.
4. The total catch of the (fisherman) _____ consisted of seven legal-sized (trout) _____.
5. The (alumna) _____ raised enough money to build three (laboratory) _____.
6. The (half) _____ of the (loaf) _____ of bread on top of the kitchen counters were left over from the party.
7. He produced the missing (page proof) _____ and asked us to be (witness) _____.
8. The work (crew) _____ were digging (ditch) _____ all day.
9. Do you pay (tax) _____ in the states on both your mailing and resident (address) _____?

10. All the neighborhood (busybody) _____ were talking about the expected multiple (birth) _____.

J. Write the singular form of each of the following.

1. stepsons
2. theses
3. curricula
4. mackerel
5. fathers-in-law
6. addenda
7. yourselves
8. crises
9. midwives
10. data
11. oases
12. alumnae
13. bacteria
14. mesdames

K. Write the plural form of each of the following words.

1. minx
2. knife
3. tobacco
4. wolf
5. lily
6. country
7. play
8. potato
9. family
10. cinema
11. firefighter
12. basketful
13. Susanna
14. Tuesday
15. cargo
16. r
17. &
18. 6
19. grocery
20. sieve
21. copy
22. cuff
23. wharf
24. enemy
25. series
26. deer
27. ox
28. police officer
29. IOU
30. B.S.
31. antique
32. splash
33. synopsis
34. pony
35. thief
36. sky

5. CONTRACTIONS AND POSSESSIVES

In Chapter 4 we saw that the apostrophe was used to form some plurals. This chapter turns to the two most frequent and important uses of the apostrophe: to take the place of missing letters in contractions and, followed by an *s*, to indicate ownership in possessives.

In this chapter you will learn rules for using the apostrophe when:

1. forming contractions
2. forming possessives

Take the following pretest to determine your ability to handle the apostrophe. The rules and exercises that follow will help you develop your ability in any areas where you need practice.

PRETEST

A. Write a contraction for each of the following sets of words. If you have trouble with this section, plan to study contractions on pages 62 and 63.

1. it should not
2. you can not
3. we are
4. they will
5. she is
6. he would
7. I have
8. they have not
9. we were not
10. she had not
11. it is
12. it is not
13. I am
14. I am not

B. Insert apostrophes where needed in each of the following sentences. If you have trouble with this section, plan to study contractions on pages 62 and 63.

1. Dont use abbreviations in letters. Its better to spell words out.
2. Hell be going if she isnt able to go instead.
3. In the 20s workers werent protected by Social Security.
4. Wed have gone to the museum if theyd shown a film there.
5. Whos going to the circus? The elephantsll be there.
6. Im sure it was hers before it was yours.

C. Write the possessive form of each noun in italics. If you have trouble with this section, plan to study rules for showing possession on pages 64 through 67.

1. the uniforms of the *team*   the _____ uniforms
2. the notice given in a *moment*   a _____ notice
3. the portrait of the *princess*   the _____ portrait
4. the rights of a *citizen*   a _____ rights
5. the role of the *actress*   the _____ role
6. the promises of some *politicians*   some _____ promises
7. the pond of the *geese*   the _____ pond
8. the names of the *children*   the _____ names
9. the luggage of the *travelers*   the _____ luggage
10. the decision of the *candidates*   the _____ decision
11. the appointment of *Charles*   _____ appointment
12. the route of the *bus*   the _____ route
13. the poems of *Robert Frost*   _____ poems
14. the association of *sports writers*   the _____ association

CONTRACTIONS

A contraction is a word that is formed when two words are combined and one or more of their letters are left out. The apostrophe takes the place of the missing letter or letters.

Contractions and Possessives / 63

is not	isn't	(the apostrophe takes the place of the missing *o* in not)
let us	let's	(the apostrophe takes the place of the missing *u* in us)
it is	it's	(the apostrophe takes the place of the missing *i* in is)
I have	I've	(the apostrophe takes the place of the missing *ha* in have)

Sometimes the apostrophe is used to take the place of missing numbers:

1776—'76   1849—'49   1920s—'20s

NOTE: There is a tendency to confuse the contraction *it's* with the possessive pronoun *its*. When you can substitute the words "it is" you must use the apostrophe. When you cannot substitute the words "it is," the apostrophe is incorrect.

It's hot. (It is hot.)
The cat is licking its fur. (The cat is *not* licking *it is* fur. Therefore, no apostrophe.)

We will have more to say about possessives on pages 64 through 67.

EXERCISE 1: Write a contraction for each of the following.

1. I have
2. she will
3. that is
4. who is
5. I will
6. they are
7. it is
8. 1984
9. where is
10. I would not
11. you are
12. do not
13. we are
14. does not
15. will not
16. he is
17. what is
18. are not
19. must have
20. should have

Mastering Spelling

EXERCISE 2: In the following sentences, some contractions are missing apostrophes and some contractions have incorrectly placed apostrophes. Rewrite the incorrect contractions.

1. I wouldve done it on time if theyd given me sufficient notice.
2. Were going to leave on time today.
3. Have'nt you noticed its' nearly time to leave?
4. Youl'l definitely hear from me.
5. Whats the time limit for the contest?
6. Thats' a decision the judgesll have to make.
7. Shes a member of the class of 53.
8. Youre just in time for dinner.
9. Its too bad that theyv'e gone already.
10. Im sure Ill never reheat anything if they come back later.

POSSESSION

The other major use of the apostrophe is to show possession. Usually an *s* follows the apostrophe, but sometimes the apostrophe is used alone. The rules that follow should make clear the use of the apostrophe to show possession.

RULE 1: To show possession for singular nouns

Add *'s* to all singular nouns, including nouns that end in *s*.

    the lady's glove   somebody's umbrella
    the chair's cushion   the boss's office

Singular nouns that end with an "s" sound (but not with the letter *s*) become possessive with the addition of only an apostrophe (').

    experience' sake   conscience' decision

RULE 2: To show possession for plural nouns

Add *'s* to all plural nouns that do not end in *s*. (That is, most irregular plural nouns take *'s*.)

Contractions and Possessives / 65

men's hats   mice's tails   alumni's meetings

BUT: Add only an apostrophe (') to plural nouns that end in *s*. (That is, most regular plurals take only apostrophe.)

boys' camp   trains' engines   Eskimos' carvings

RULE 3: To show possession for proper nouns that end in *s*

When a proper noun, including a name, ends in *s*, you may add either *'s* or *'* alone to show possession.

James's desk *or* James' desk   Dickens's works *or* Dickens' works

However, by custom, some names ending in *s* use only the apostrophe (') to show possession.

    Moses' laws   Euripides' characters
    Jesus' disciples   Ramses' pyramids

EXERCISE 3: Make the following phrases possessive.

1. the hats of the bosses
2. the skill of the pilot
3. the voice of the woman
4. the voices of the men
5. the shoes of the men
6. the work of the women
7. the hair of the lass
8. the fur of the cats
9. the desk of Charles
10. the pen of Maurice
11. the sermons of Jesus
12. the scent of incense

RULE 4: To show possession for compound words

To show possession for word groups or compound words, add *'s* to the last word in the group.

    my son-in-law's house   someone else's car
    the editor-in-chief's typewriter   Jack Hartley, Sr.'s lawn

RULE 5: To show possession for more than one individual

To show possession for each individual when two or more are named, add *'s* to each name.

>Bill's and Harry's stores

In this example, the word *stores* is plural: the store owned by Bill and the store owned by Harry. But if Bill and Harry were partners and jointly owned a single store, show possession according to Rule 3 above.

>Bill and Harry's store

For another example,

>Gilbert and Sullivan's operettas

indicates the result of a collaboration by the librettist and the composer, while

>Offenbach's and Bizet's operas

indicates the separate works of the two composers.

RULE 6: To show duration of time

A similar use of the apostrophe, although not strictly possession, refers to close relationships or the duration of time, and follows the above rules.

>a week's wages   three months' delay

EXERCISE 4: Make the following possessive.

1. coat of your brother-in-law
2. the hat of Samuel Cooper, Jr.
3. the house of Sara and John
4. the tablecloth of someone
5. the bikes of Carol and Anna
6. the flowers of Stanislaus
7. the pen of the commander-in-chief
8. the benefits of dependents
9. the work of two days
10. the union of electricians

Contractions and Possessives / 67

11. the judgments of Moses
12. a vacation lasting three weeks
13. the gowns of the ladies-in-waiting
14. the desks of the schools
15. the office of Dean Harris

RULE 7: Possessive nouns

NEVER use an apostrophe with the possessive pronouns *yours, his, hers, its, ours, theirs, whose.*

>   The trunk is yours.   His clothes are here.

NOTE: You will not confuse *whose* and *who's* if you remember that *who's* is the contraction of *who is.*
>   Who's that?   (Who is that?)
>   Whose is that?   (Who owns that? *not* Who is is that?)

EXERCISE 5: Correct the errors in the following sentences.

1. Who'se going to the birthday party?
2. You're friends aren't invited but her's are.
3. Its going to be a fancy affair.
4. Whose driving?
5. Let's take our car, not their's.
6. They're presents are wrapped. Our's are not.

EXERCISE 6: Rewrite the following phrases, using apostrophes where needed.

1. a drivers license
2. puppies tails
3. a scouts honor
4. the presidents advisors
5. yours and theirs
6. an officers medals
7. five days work
8. a clubs members

9. a 65 Ford Mustang
10. musics appeal
11. theyre the best
12. its paw
13. foxes tails
14. womens department
15. whose cousins
16. plumbers union
17. churchs steeple
18. Americans eating habits
19. cities leaders
20. fishermens cove

EXERCISES FOR REVIEW

A. Write the contraction of each phrase.

1. would not
2. you will
3. I am
4. they would
5. you are
6. I have not
7. it is
8. must not
9. I have
10. does not
11. we can not
12. they should not
13. he has not
14. I am not
15. they will
16. she has
17. it is not
18. he had

B. Complete the following sentences with a contraction of the phrase in parentheses.

1. I (can not) _____ go with you.
2. (She will) _____ give you your books if (they are) _____ ready.
3. We (are not) _____ able to decide (who will) _____ be our representative.
4. The lion (had not) _____ left its den for weeks.

5. (It is) _____ almost five o'clock.
6. (When will) _____ dinner be ready?
7. The students (will not) _____ be able to wait much longer.
8. Already (they are) _____ clamoring to enter the dining room.
9. (Do they not) _____ want to know (what is) _____ on the menu?
10. I think (they have) _____ asked but they (have not) _____ been given an answer.

C. Make the following phrases possessive.

1. the umbrellas of the women
2. the collars of the dogs
3. the desks of the children
4. the kite of Dolores
5. the cage of the monkey
6. the hats of the bosses
7. the tablets of Moses
8. the checks for the month
9. the tracks for the race cars
10. the decision of the judges

D. Make the following compound words and word groups possessive.

1. the house of your mother-in-law
2. the lawn of someone else
3. the car of Jack Parsons, Sr.
4. the desk of the executive secretary
5. the tent of May and Bill
6. the tents of May and of Bill
7. the calendar of the editor-in-chief
8. the garden of my step-daughter
9. the lamp of someone
10. the leave-of-absence of Mark

E. Rewrite the incorrect words in the following sentences.

1. Its time for the drama classs readings.
2. I'm for Thomas plan when were permitted to vote.
3. All the singers voices blended.
4. The first singers voice is the strongest.
5. Marys' illustration is better than Joes'.
6. Who'se there?
7. Deniss concern for my welfare is not as sincere as yours'.
8. This is her's.
9. The other one is our's.
10. Jacks and Susans houses are for sale.

F. Read the following and make the necessary corrections.

Some years' ago, a society hostess named Mrs. Morrow invited the famous J. P. Morgan for tea. She was nervous. Mr. Morgans nose was very large. He was sensitive to peoples stares. So everyone hed ever known carefully avoided staring at his' nose. Of course, no one ever mentioned it, not even people who's noses were as big as his'.

Mrs. Morrows two small daughters nurse was going to meet Mr. Morgan at the tea and she asked to bring the little girls with her. The little girls were warned not to look at their mothers friends nose. Theyd been warned many times.

The day of the tea came. The little girls, accompanied by they're nurse, came into the room. Who'se going to make a mistake, Mrs. Morrow wondered. "Ive brought the children to meet you," the nurse said. Mr. Morgans smile was friendly. Everything had gone very well. The children left, and the butler, who's manners were perfect, brought in the tea.

Mrs. Morrows relief was enormous. She was happy. She turned to her famous guest and said, "And now, Mr. Morgan, will you have cream or lemon in you're nose?"

6. CHANGING FORMS OF WORDS

"When *I* use a word," says the character Humpty Dumpty in *Through the Looking-Glass* by Lewis Carroll, "it means just what I choose it to mean—neither more nor less." One way we get words to express our exact meanings is by changing their forms. To change word forms we add suffixes and prefixes that make our words, like Humpty Dumpty's, mean exactly what we want them to mean. Thus, the verb *edit* becomes the noun *editor* when you add the suffix *-or*. The verb *agree* becomes the adjective *agreeable* when you add the suffix *-able*.

You can also change the meaning of a word by adding a prefix. The word *agreeable* becomes its opposite, *disagreeable*, when you add the prefix *dis-*.

Changing word forms can lead to spelling problems. Many suffix groups have similar meanings and pronunciations, but are spelled differently. When do you add *-or* and when *-er*? What about *-ent* and *-ant*? Prefixes can give you spelling headaches too. When do you use *de-* or *di-*, *in-* or *un-*, *dis-*, *mis-*, *il-*, *ir-* . . . ?

This chapter comes to your rescue, with explanations and exercises to give you practice in choosing the right spelling for the word form you want. In this chapter you will practice spelling words formed when:

1. suffixes are used to change adjectives and verbs to nouns
2. suffixes form adjectives from nouns and verbs
3. suffixes change adjectives into adverbs
4. an adjective is derived from the name of a nation or geographical unit
5. prefixes are used to create antonyms

After reading these explanations and doing these exercises, you should be more confident about spelling the changed forms of many words. For those words that still give you problems, you will know the possible choices. Then you will be able to check the possibilities—*-ence* or *-ance?*—in your dictionary. Once you understand the patterns used in the English language to make new words from their basic forms, you will be well on the way to correct spelling of many troublesome words.

FORMING NOUNS

There are suffixes that can change adjectives and verbs to nouns. Other suffixes will even change nouns to other nouns with slightly different meanings. In this section, we'll look at how to spell the words formed in these ways.

Changing Adjectives to Nouns

The suffixes -*ty*, -*ity*, and -*ness* change an adjective to a noun that means "the state or condition of being." In some cases a final or other letter from the basic word is changed or dropped.

      cruel—cruelty   generous—generosity
      sudden—suddenness   hardy—hardiness

    (You may want to review the rules for spelling words ending in *y* when suffixes are added; see page 28.)

EXERCISE 1: Change the adjectives listed below to noun forms ending in -*ty*, -*ity*, or -*ness*.

1. pleasant
2. lax
3. petty
4. open-minded
5. wordy
6. sensitive
7. gay
8. mature
9. stubborn
10. hearty
11. noisy
12. loud
13. firm
14. royal
15. happy

Changing Verbs to Nouns (and Nouns to Verbs)

The suffixes -*er* and -*or* change verbs to noun forms that mean "a person who performs the action."

        buy—buyer   sail—sailor

When you add *-er* or *-or*, drop the silent *e* at the end of the word.

advise—adviser *or* advisor

EXERCISE 2: Change the following verb forms to noun forms ending in *-er* or *-or*.

1. act
2. announce
3. operate
4. edit
5. report
6. inspect
7. govern
8. import
9. manage
10. supervise
11. teach
12. invent
13. senate
14. profess
15. employ

The suffixes *-ance* and *-ence* change verbs into noun forms that mean "the act of" or "the state of being." When adding these suffixes, drop the silent *e* at the end of the verb. Also, refer to the doubling rule on page 39.

resist—resistance   occur—occurrence   insure—insurance

EXERCISE 3: Change the following verb forms to noun forms ending in *-ance* or *-ence*.

1. refer
2. accord
3. excel
4. depend
5. attend
6. correspond
7. interfere
8. prefer
9. allow
10. deter
11. accept
12. persevere
13. confer
14. assist
15. reside

The suffixes *-ion*, *-tion*, *-sion*, or *-ation* change verbs into noun forms that mean "the act of" or "the state of being." Note that one or more final letters of the verb may have to be dropped or changed.

separate—separation   expand—expansion
admire—admiration   concede—concession
decline—declension   expel—expulsion

Changing Forms of Words / 75

EXERCISE 4: Change the following verb forms into nouns by adding the suffixes *-ion, -tion, -sion,* or *-ation*. Change the spelling as needed. If you can't figure out how to make the *-ion* noun form, consult your dictionary.

1. convert
2. limit
3. adore
4. compress
5. extend
6. terminate
7. sense
8. diffuse
9. transmit
10. imagine
11. permit
12. persuade
13. succeed
14. condescend
15. divide
16. ignite
17. execute
18. comprehend
19. possess
20. revert
21. propel
22. permit
23. expand
24. explode

Removal of the suffixes discussed in this section restores the verb form. In some cases simply dropping the suffix will do. In other cases some letters in the basic verb form will have to be changed.

    admission—admit   resistance—resist

EXERCISE 5: Remove the suffix of the following noun forms to restore the basic verb form. You may have to change or add a letter. Consult your dictionary if necessary.

1. repetition
2. addition
3. toleration
4. retention
5. perception
6. resumption
7. institution
8. conversion
9. attendance
10. acceptance
11. conference
12. correspondence
13. omission
14. experimentation
15. calculation

Changing Nouns to Another Noun Form

The suffixes *-ist* or *-ian* can be added to some nouns to form a different noun meaning "the person who does, works with, or is skilled at." In some cases the final letter may have to be dropped or changed.

    mathematics—mathematician   piano—pianist   library—librarian

EXERCISE 6: Change each of the following nouns to a different noun form by adding the suffix *-ist* or *-ian*. Consult your dictionary if necessary.

music   machine   science
guard   solo   violin
art   journal   history
electric   cello   seminary
colony   special   grammar

FORMING OTHER PARTS OF SPEECH

Suffixes can transform nouns and verbs into adjectives; adjectives into adverbs; and verbs into participles which can be used as nouns or verbs. We'll look at all of these changed word forms in this section.

Forming Adjectives

The suffixes *-al* and *-ial* are used to change many nouns into adjectives. As with many other suffix constructions, a final letter may have to be changed or dropped.

    accident—accidental   confidence—confidential

EXERCISE 7: Change the following nouns into adjectives by adding the suffix *-al* or *-ial*. Consult your dictionary if necessary.

1. potent
2. incident
3. origin
4. continent
5. sensation
6. orient
7. reverent
8. coincidence
9. exception
10. experiment
11. person
12. influence
13. occasion
14. president
15. penitence

    Adjectives can also be formed by adding the suffix *-able* or *-ible* to many nouns and verbs.

        sale (noun)—saleable (adjective)
        contempt (noun)—contemptible (adjective)
        believe (verb)—believable (adjective)

EXERCISE 8: Change the following words to adjectives by adding the suffix *-able* or *-ible*. Consult your dictionary if necessary.

1. compare
2. advise
3. believe
4. response
5. conceive
6. reason
7. force
8. notice
9. favor
10. allow
11. return
12. laugh
13. agree
14. comfort
15. change

The suffixes *-ary* and *-ory* change nouns and verbs to nouns or adjectives meaning "that which, one who, place where, or pertaining to." Note that some letters may have to be dropped or changed.

satisfy (verb)—satisfactory (noun)
custom (noun)—customary (adjective)

EXERCISE 9: Change the following nouns and verbs to nouns or adjectives by adding the suffix *-ary* or *-ory*. Consult your dictionary if necessary.

1. congratulate
2. direct
3. advise
4. second
5. revolution
6. deposit
7. sense
8. dispense

Forming Adverbs

An adverb is usually formed by adding the suffix *-ly* to an adjective form.

actual—actually   merry—merrily

EXERCISE 10: Write the adverb form of each of the following adjectives. Check the doubling rule on page 39.

1. final
2. lucky
3. necessary
4. particular
5. original
6. steady

7. hasty	8. busy	9. immediate
10. according	11. sincere	12. heavy
13. easy	14. satisfactory	15. exact

Changing Verbs to Other Word Forms

A verb can become an adjective or a noun by the addition of the suffix *-ent* or *-ant,* meaning "one who is or does, that which is or does, or the state of being."

>depend—dependent (noun *or* adjective)
>urge—urgent (adjective)
>serve—servant (noun)

Note that a final letter may have to be dropped or doubled.

EXERCISE 11: Change each of the following verbs to a noun or adjective by adding the suffix *-ent* or *-ant.* Check the doubling rule on page 39, and consult your dictionary if necessary.

1. attend	2. superintend	3. depend
4. please	5. confide	6. import
7. combat	8. disinfect	9. correspond
10. assist	11. preside	12. differ
13. resist	14. excel	15. reside

Addition of the suffix *-ing* turns the infinitive form of a verb into the present participle. Note that a final letter may be dropped or doubled.

>dance—dancing   occur—occurring   buy—buying

Remember that the present participle can be used in three ways:
1. to indicate present or continuing action:
   We are dancing.
2. as an adjective:
   The circus displayed dancing bears.

3. as a noun:

Aerobic dancing has become a popular exercise.

EXERCISE 12: Change each of the following verb forms into its present participle by adding the suffix -*ing*. Check the doubling rule on page 39.

1. notice	2. slip	3. begin
4. hit	5. come	6. greet
7. provide	8. bathe	9. drop
10. dine	11. believe	12. fly
13. make	14. trim	15. refer

The Adjective Forms of Geographical Names

The name of a nation or other geographical unit can become a noun or adjective form that refers to the inhabitants, customs, and/or language of that place. The most usual suffixes used for this purpose are -*n*, -*an*, and -*ian*. In some cases a final letter is dropped or changed.

America—American   Mexico—Mexican
Iran—Iranian   Peru—Peruvian
California—Californian   India—Indian

EXERCISE 13: Write the adjective form of the following countires or other geographical units. Note that the adjectives are also capitalized.

1. Cuba	2. Russia	3. Brazil
4. Morocco	5. Korea	6. Czechoslovakia
7. Panama	8. Canada	9. Italy
10. Africa	11. Asia	12. Hungary
13. Germany	14. Kansas	15. Sahara

Some adjective forms of geographical units are formed by the addition of the suffixes -*ese* and -*ish*. Note that various letter changes may be required.

Japan—Japanese   England—English
Portugal—Portuguese   Denmark—Danish

Note too that some *-ian* forms require unusual letter changes:

    Belgium—Belgian   Norway—Norwegian

Other forms derived from place names are irregular, and may be based on local custom or the language of the country.

Israel—Israeli
Greece—Greek
Michigan—Michigander
Quebec—Quebecois(e)
France—French
Iceland—Icelandic
Switzerland—Swiss

New York—New Yorker
Maryland—Marylander
Turkey—Turk (people), Turkish (language)
Holland *or* Netherlands—Dutch
Los Angeles—Angeleño
Yemen—Yemenite

EXERCISE 14: Write the noun or adjective form of the following countries or other geographical units. Consult your dictionary if necessary.

1. Sweden
2. Poland
3. Burma
4. China
5. Scotland
6. New Zealand
7. Spain
8. Vietnam
9. Ceylon
10. Iraq
11. Thailand
12. Berlin

USING PREFIXES TO FORM ANTONYMS

The following prefixes all have the meaning of "not": *un-, im-, in-, il-, ir-, dis-, mis-*.

Each of these negative prefixes can be used to change a word to its antonym or opposite.

    like—unlike   prove—disprove
    direct—indirect   probable—improbable

Note that adding a negative prefix does *not* change the word to a different part of speech. An adjective becomes another adjective with the opposite meaning. A verb becomes another verb with the opposite meaning.

    compatible—incompatible (adjective)
    possess—dispossess (verb)

Changing Forms of Words / 81

There are some patterns that will help. The most common of these negative prefixes is *un-*, which is used most often to form adjectives:

        unlikely   unsuitable

But *un-* is also used to form verbs:

        unsettle   undo

Most commonly used to create negative verb forms is *dis-*:

        disembark   disagree

But *dis-* can also be used in adjectives and nouns:

        discontent   discord

Use *mis-* to form negative nouns or verbs:

        misfortune   misrepresent

Before a word that begins with the letter *r* the prefix *ir* is most often used; before a word that begins with the letter *l* the prefix *il-* is most often used:

        irradiate   illegible

Use *im-* before words beginning with *a, b, i, m, p:*

   imbalance   immature   improper

Use *in-* with almost any letter:

   inability   indefinite   insane

DO NOT confuse *in-*, meaning "not," with *in-* meaning "into":

   inmost   inflight   inside

EXERCISE 15: Change the meaning of each of the following words to its antonym by adding the prefix *un-, im-, in-, il-, ir-, dis-,* or *mis-*. Consult your dictionary if necessary.

1. important
2. legal
3. active
4. regular
5. pleased
6. responsible
7. capable
8. understand
9. approve
10. happy
11. respectful
12. agreeable
13. pleasant
14. perfect
15. possible

EXERCISES FOR REVIEW

A. Change the following adjectives to nouns by adding one of the following suffixes: *-ty, -ity, -ness*.

1. profound
2. round
3. full
4. grandiose
5. tough
6. tender
7. tangy
8. wary
9. trustworthy
10. single-minded
11. scarce
12. vain

B. Change the following words to mean a person who performs the action by adding the suffixes *-er, -or, -ist*, or *-ian*. Change the spelling if necessary.

1. sail
2. advertise
3. type
4. magic
5. biology
6. instruct
7. custom
8. statistic
9. perform
10. paint
11. fly
12. language

C. Change the following verb forms to noun forms by adding the suffixes *-ence, -ance, -ion, -tion, -sion*, or *-ation*. You may have to drop or change one or more final letters.

1. evade
2. substitute
3. remember
4. depend
5. appear
6. submerge
7. pretend
8. acquaint
9. remit
10. confess
11. revere
12. regress
13. demonstrate
14. calculate
15. mortify

D. Change the following noun forms into verb forms.

1. apprehension
2. collision
3. interference
4. conclusion
5. immersion
6. intention
7. adherence
8. oppression
9. fortification

Changing Forms of Words / 83

10. adoration 11. dependence 12. performance

E. Change the following word forms to adjectives by adding the suffixes -able, -ible, -al, or -ial.

1. form
2. intention
3. excusable
4. prime
5. advise
6. value
7. excuse
8. suit
9. family
10. move
11. stop
12. afford

F. Write the adverb form of each of the following adjectives by adding the suffix -ly.

1. definite
2. practical
3. natural
4. annual
5. frequent
6. hasty
7. cordial
8. formal
9. awful
10. former
11. entire
12. happy

G. Change the following verb forms into adjective or noun forms by adding the suffixes -ent or -ant.

1. insist
2. depend
3. urge
4. resist
5. consist
6. result
7. state
8. correspond
9. assist
10. precede
11. differ
12. attend

H. Change each of the following verb forms into its present participle, the -ing form. The final letter may have to be dropped or doubled.

1. dig
2. mine
3. graduate
4. lose
5. implore
6. commit
7. extol
8. revolve
9. circle
10. break
11. lurch
12. startle

I. Write the adjective form of each of the following place names.

1. Switzerland
2. Mexico
3. Kenya
4. France
5. Jordan
6. Ireland
7. Jamaica
8. Bolivia
9. Israel
10. Puerto Rico
11. Australia
12. Brazil
13. Portugal
14. Belgium
15. Norway
16. Denmark
17. Scotland
18. Japan
19. Amazon
20. Nebraska
21. Greece

J. Change the meaning of the following words by adding one of these prefixes: *un-, im-, in-, ir-, dis-, mis-*.

1. probable
2. direct
3. agreeable
4. active
5. fair
6. honest
7. dependent
8. valuable
9. correct
10. natural
11. fortunate
12. religious

7. PROBLEMS WITH PREFIXES AND HYPHENS

Chapter 6 was devoted to suffixes that change word forms and meanings, and prefixes used to form antonyms. This chapter explains how to avoid spelling errors when writing some other commonly used prefixes. It also examines the use of the hyphen in forming compound words.

In this chapter you will learn:

1. the meanings of some commonly confused prefixes and how to spell them
2. spelling rules for one important group of words formed with prefixes
3. how to form compound words with and without hyphens

SPELLINGS AND USES OF COMMON PREFIXES

The Prefixes *pre-* and *per-*

It's easy to confuse words beginning with *pre-* and *per-*. Sonetimes knowing the meanings of these prefixes can help: *per-* means "before" or "at an earlier time"; *pre-* means "through, throughout, away, thoroughly, completely."

        prepay—to pay in advance
        perfume—filled (through) with a pleasing odor

Generally, if the meaning "before" fits the word, *pre-* is probably the correct spelling. For example, *premedical* refers to courses taken before the formal study of medicine begins. But in many "pre-" words knowing the prefix meaning will not be much of a guide. The only way to know how to spell *premium, present, pretend* and others is to see them, to say them, and to remember them.

86 / Mastering Spelling

This goes for the "per-" words as well. You may *percolate* your coffee, *perspire* when you jog too fast, and plant *perennial* flowers in your garden. Look at the words, say them carefully—and try to remember the pronunciation. If you say these words carefully, you should have no difficulty in deciding which spelling to use.

EXERCISE 1: In each pair below circle the word that is *incorrectly* spelled.

1. predict/preceive
2. pertain/pertend
3. perdiction/perdition
4. present/presecute
5. persume/persist
6. perserve/preserve
7. persent/present
8. preplexing/perplexing
9. perspective/prospective
10. premit/permit

The Prefixes *for-* and *fore-*

Pronunciation will not help with this pair of prefixes, but knowing the meaning might. The prefix *for-* means "away, apart, against, off." The prefix *fore-* means "in, at the front of, in advance of."

        forbid—to rule or order against
        foretell—to announce in advance, to predict

EXERCISE 2: Complete the spelling of each of the following words by adding the prefix *for-* or *fore-*.

1. _____runner
2. _____most
3. _____give
4. _____head
5. _____get
6. _____go
7. _____see
8. _____sake
9. _____hand

The Prefix *dis-*

The prefix *dis-* has several forms:

1. *dis-* becomes *di-* before the letters *b, d, g, l, m, n, r, v*

                diverge   dilute

2. *dis-* sometimes becomes *dif-* before the letter *f*

diffuse

The prefix *dis-* (*di-, dif-*) has the following meanings when it is used to create verbs:

>dismiss—away or apart
>disfigure—make the opposite of
>disbar—deprive of or expel from
>disappear, disallow—fail, cease, **refuse to**
>disjoin—reverse the action of

The prefix *dis-* also means "not, the opposite of" when it is used to form adjectives:

dishonest

The prefix *dis-* also means "opposite of" or "lack of" when it is used to form nouns:

disunion   disease

EXERCISE 3: Complete the following words by adding *dis-, di-,* or *dif-* as necessary.

1. _____connect
2. _____satisfy
3. _____claimer
4. _____infect
5. _____vorce
6. _____ulate
7. _____fuse
8. _____use
9. _____locate

NOTE: The *di-* form of the prefix *dis-* should not be confused with the prefix *di*, meaning "twice, twofold, doubled":

diatomic   dichotomy   dioxide

The Prefix *de-*

The prefix *de-* has some of the same meanings as *dis-*:

>derail—away or apart from, off
>decode—reverse the action of

In addition, *de-* can mean "down, decline, entirely, or debug."

88 / Mastering Spelling

EXERCISE 4: Complete the following words by adding *dis-, di-, dif-,* or *de-*. Use your dictionary if necessary.

1. _____service
2. _____courage
3. _____press
4. _____enchant
5. _____tour
6. _____duct
7. _____allow
8. _____compose
9. _____entangle
10. _____spite
11. _____segregate
12. _____program

The *-sede, -ceed,* and *-cede* Words

When do you *proceed* and when *precede*? You can actually *do* both at once, but you had better spell them differently! To get the spelling right, you have to know your prefixes *and* the Latin word *cedere*, "to go." Let's take a closer look at a confusing group of words.

1. First, the *-ceed* and *-cede* words should not be confused with any sound-alikes. There is only one English word that ends in *-sede*:

supersede

The *sede* root is from the Latin word *sedere*, "to sit." Literally, *supersede* means "to sit on top of"; it is used to mean "to be used in place of."

The new spelling textbook will supersede the one we used last year.

2. Only three English words end in the *-ceed* form of *cedere*:

exceed—to go more *or* to do more
proceed—to go forward
succeed—to go afterward

Note that these words form the following:

excessive (adjective)   procession (noun)   succession (noun)
                      procedure (noun)

3. All other English words in this group use the root form *cede*:

accede—to go to, to agree with   recede—to go back
concede—to go with or give in   precede—to go before
intercede—to go between   secede—to go away from

Note that the words in this group form the following nouns:

accession   recession
concession   precedence
intercession   secession

Each prefix is used with only one of this group of roots. Therefore, if you learn the four prefixes in Rules 1 and 2 above—*super-*, *ex-*, *pro-*, and *suc-*—your spelling problems with this group of words will be solved: Any other prefix goes with *-cede*.

EXERCISE 5: Fill in the blanks in the following paragraphs using *-sede, -ceed, -cede, -cession,* or *-cedence*. (You may have to use the past tense form of some verbs.)

When I began acting, I pro_____ very logically. I went to several auditions in suc_____. But wherever I went, it seemed I had just been pre_____ by someone whose talents super_____ mine. A friend said he would inter_____ for me with a famous director. "The theater is in a deep re_____," the director told me dramatically. "You will have to make many con_____ in order to get your start. Now, if you will pre_____ me up the stairs, we will see what you can do."

I read, I sang, I even danced a little. The director seemed impressed. "If you ac_____ to these terms, perhaps I can find a part for you," she said. I was thrilled—until I looked at the contract! When I saw how little I would be paid, I wanted to se_____ from the theater!

FORMING COMPOUND WORDS

The hyphen is used to form some compound words.

> My sister is a non-conformist.
> Do you know my brother-in-law?

There is, however, a trend toward using fewer hyphens. Many words that used to be hyphenated are no longer hyphenated. When in doubt, it is best to consult the dictionary. The following rules should serve as guidelines:

1. Compound numbers from twenty-one to ninety-nine are hyphenated.

    sixty-three   eighty-eight

BUT: nineteen   one hundred and one

2. Use a hyphen when a noun is used as an adjective.

    student-manager   soldier-ambassador

BUT: major general

3. Use a hyphen in an adjective of two or more words if it precedes the noun modified.

    three-year-old child   one-time fee

4. Use a hyphen to separate a prefix from a proper noun.

    pro-British   un-American

5. Use a hyphen in compounds of three or more words.

    brother-in-law   give-and-take

BUT: stepbrother   breakthrough   dining room

Do NOT use a hyphen for the following:

1. points of the compass

    northeast   southwest

2. combinations of words with *any, every, some*

    anybody   everywhere   something

3. combinations of the word *no* with *body, thing,* and *where*

    nobody   nothing   nowhere

4. The following are always written as separate words:

    all right   no one

Be accurate when you use hyphens, since a misplaced hyphen can change the meaning of a word, phrase, or sentence. The following sentences illustrate this point.

1. Jack is a first-class manager.
Jack is our first class-manager.
2. Bert is running on a ticket to reform the district.
The district is being re-formed as a result of re-districting.

3. Don't eat that half-raw chicken.
   Here's a half raw chicken for you to cook.
4. I ordered four-color photos.
   Here's an envelope for the four color photos you ordered.

EXERCISE 6: In the following phrases insert hyphens or indicate an unhyphenated compound (bedroom) where necessary.

1. a fifty dollar suit
2. a suit for fifty dollars
3. two thirds
4. forty hour week
5. every thing is here
6. book worm
7. ten cent book
8. pro French
9. step son
10. one time leader
11. well dressed student
12. full grown monster
13. fifty five
14. all right
15. north east corner
16. every where
17. some thing
18. no body
19. pleasant looking boy
20. sail boat
21. no where
22. twenty nine

EXERCISES FOR REVIEW

A. Use *ante-, anti-, pre-, per-, for-,* or *fore-* to complete the spelling of the indicated words.

1. Her letter was a _____runner of more bad news.
2. He pointed with his _____finger.
3. It was feared that the enemy would _____vail.
4. The doctor brought the _____dote to the poison.
5. He is simply shy, not _____social.
6. What did he _____dict the outcome would be?
7. The team had to _____feit the game because of weather.
8. If you lie under oath you have committed _____jury.

9. _____mit me to introduce myself.
10. The bronze door is at the _____rior (situated near the front) of the church.
11. _____warned, they say, is _____armed.
12. One justice's argument was the _____thesis of the other's.
13. If we _____pare the agenda everyone will know what will be done at the meeting.
14. She came to seek her _____tune.
15. The door to the _____room was locked.

B. Use *dis-*, *di-*, *dif-*, or *de-* to complete the spelling of the indicated words.

1. Magicians are always making rabbits _____appear.
2. Some people think it pays to be _____honest.
3. I think they are doing themselves a _____service.
4. How did the _____pute begin?
5. The president broke the tie with a _____senting vote.
6. That quickly _____tracted from the spirit of harmony in the room.
7. The situation _____clined rapidly after that.
8. Soon everyone was making _____mands.
9. There must be better ways to deal with honest _____ferences of opinion.
10. I'm glad I'm not so _____pendent on the opinions of other people.
11. A _____versity of ideas is healthy.
12. After all, you can't _____vorce yourself from the issues of your time.

C. Use *sede*, *ceed*, or *cede* to complete the spelling of the indicated words.

1. Will he ever suc_____ in learning to play chess?
2. Who will super_____ the governor's order?

3. The waters re_____d from the high water mark set during the hurricane.
4. Management refused to con_____ to the union's demands.
5. Their demands did ex_____ the company's ability to pay.
6. Still, the bosses might have ac_____d to some of the points.
7. Her visit pre_____d his by three hours.
8. The founders never dreamed that any state would want to se_____ from the United States.
9. You will pro_____ with the contingency plan.
10. The students asked their instructor to inter_____ for them.

D. In the following phrases, insert hyphens or indicate one-word compounds where necessary.

1. hanger on
2. runner up
3. city state
4. to and fro motion
5. non orthodox
6. seventy five
7. pleasant looking boy
8. fear filled hours
9. far flung troops
10. any thing
11. all right
12. pro democracy
13. will o' the wisp
14. never to be forgotten days
15. south eastern states
16. half hearted answer
17. loud mouthed leader
18. twenty year old student
19. four minute mile
20. athletic looking woman

8. PRONUNCIATION HELPS AND HINDRANCES

Many people spell phonetically. That is, they try to spell every word the way it sounds. This often works: If you pronounce many words correctly, you are indeed quite likely to spell them correctly too. On the other hand, incorrect pronunciation may well lead to incorrect spelling. But there are many words for which correct pronunciation does not guarantee correct spelling. And there are many English words that contain a "silent letter" that must be written although it is not pronounced.

In this chapter you will learn to:

1. pronounce and spell commonly mispronounced words
2. recognize and spell sounds which can be represented by different letters
3. identify letters and letter combinations which are often pronounced differently
4. spell words which contain silent letters

COMMONLY MISPRONOUNCED WORDS

The following words are often not pronounced the way they are spelled. Say each word as you read it. (You may want to check your dictionary for the preferred pronunciation.) You may be able to remember the correct spelling better if you note the sequence of all the letters in each word as you say it. Be sure not to put in extra syllables that don't belong in the word.

library	picture	vegetable
naturally	February	veteran
preferable	accidentally	chimney
champion	general	musically
laboratory	mischievous	several
incidentally	interesting	disastrous
weight	practically	mystery
mathematics	height	diamond

EXERCISE 1: Complete the spelling of the word whose definition is given in parentheses. Check your answers. If you spell any word incorrectly, look up the pronunciation in your dictionary. Then write the word in your spelling notebook and mark the divisions between syllables. When you study these words make sure you pronounce every syllable indicated.

1. The gen_____l (common, widespread) opinion in the class is that English spelling is more complicated than Spanish.
2. The silent *k* in particular is a great mys_____y (unexplained, unknown) to me.
3. The only way Jack spells some words correctly is accident_____y (by chance), but he considers himself a champ_____n (winner of first place) speller.
4. Frankly, I'd much rather have a di_____d (valuable gemstone) than spell it.
5. On the other hand, I'd rather spell math_____tics (group of sciences dealing with numbers and symbols) than work out problems.
6. Jack mixed the wrong chemicals together and caused an explosion in the lab_____tory (place of work).
7. Did you measure the hei_____ (distance from bottom to top) and width of the box?
8. I have sev_____al (more than a few) things to do this afternoon.
9. The weather in Feb_____ry (second month in the year) can be dis_____ous (terrible).
10. Sometimes that causes int_____ing (attention-getting) problems.
11. How many p_____s (paintings, drawings, photographs) are in the book?

SOUND-ALIKES THAT ARE SPELLED DIFFERENTLY

All sounds that sound alike are not spelled alike. The sound of the letter *f*, for example, appears as *f* in the word *free*. But the sound of the letter *f* is spelled *ph* in the word *phantom*, *ff* in *cuff*, and *gh* in *rough*.

96 / Mastering Spelling

The words in each of the following groups are examples of different letters or letter combinations with the same pronunciation that are spelled in different ways:

foolish	roof	bluff
phase	ephemeral	enough
line	site	rind
align	shy	type
kite	stein	
usual	used	human
review	few	you
ape	say	away
aim	weigh	melee
gypsy	we	scene
seen	seize	cuisine
lien	lean	
through	threw	Sioux
boo	clue	

EXERCISE 2: Complete the spelling of the words whose definitions are given in parentheses. The words may sound similar, but are spelled differently. Again, check your answers. If you spell any incorrectly, add them to your spelling notebook.

1. In _____ary (second month) I start the next _____ase (part or stage) of my new job.
2. The work is t_____ (difficult) since I will be a model. But I won't be modeling clothes. I'll be posing in the bu_____ (nude) for an art class.
3. I wonder if I will be able to b_____r (endure) having everyone s_____re (look at) while I drape myself over the s_____r (step) r_____l (banister).
4. When I was ass_____ed (given) this job, I almost decl_____ed (said no) because I am so sh_____ (bashful).

5. But the personnel manager s_____d (told me) that it would be l_____s (not as much) work than some other jobs.
6. The last model told me the wind bl_____ (moved with force) so hard his skin turned bl_____ (the color)!
7. Still, I nearly thr_____ (flung away) it over because I k_____w (was sure that) I'd get pn_____monia (severe lung infection) if I had to go thr_____ (on with) that.
8. Luckily for me, the drawing class is n_____ (at this time) held indoors, so I won't have to hold the b_____ (branch) of the pine tree.
9. I'll only have to c_____ (go up) the steps this t_____ (now).

LETTER COMBINATIONS THAT ARE PRONOUNCED DIFFERENTLY

All words that look alike do not sound alike. The words *rough* and *through* end with the same letters: *ough*. Yet the words are pronounced differently. Similarly, the letter combination *ei* is pronounced *ē* in the word receive and *ā* in the word *neighbor*.

Each of the following groups of words contains the same letter combinations pronounced in different ways. Check the correct pronunciations in your dictionary if necessary.

          receipt—sleigh   pour—sour
          though—through—enough   now—stow

EXERCISE 3: Write the correct spelling of each word shown phonetically. The definitions in parentheses may help.

1. skour (to rub clean)
2. toor (to travel about)
3. bôt (purchased)
4. ruf (not smooth)
5. nā (sound made by horse)
6. sēz (capture or grab)
7. fôr (numeral after three)
8. flour (needed for bread)
9. plou (to break up the soil)
10. shō (to put on view)

SILENT LETTERS

Some letters appear in words but are often not pronounced. The letters *e, g, h, k,* and *p* are frequently silent. In addition, there are several other consonants in English words that are not always pronounced.

The letter combination *gh* is frequently silent, as in ei*gh*t and thou*gh*. (In other cases, though, as we have seen, the *gh* combination may be pronounced *f: tough*.)

Silent letters often appear in combinations in which they change the pronunciation of other letters. Thus, the silent *e* at the end of a word usually causes the preceding vowel to have a long vowel sound: sīte, appetīte. The silent *h* in *where* and *whistle* indicates that the *w* should be pronounced with a little puff of breath, unlike the "flat" *w* in *with* and *we*.

EXERCISE 4: In the space provided, write correctly the word given phonetically in parentheses.

1. What is the (rāt) _____ of pay on your new job?
2. The Ten Commandments teach us to (änər) _____ our parents.
3. The mosquitos and the (nats) _____ came to our picnic.
4. What (sīn) _____ were you born under?
5. Do you know the words to "The Marines' (him) _____?"
6. Every day he gets deeper and deeper in (det) _____.
7. The children dressed in (gōst) _____ costumes for Halloween.
8. I can't stand listening to children or dogs (hwīn) _____.
9. The cruise took them from one (īlənd) _____ to another.
10. Can you tie a square (nät) _____?
11. It was several hours before the (rek) _____ was discovered.
12. How many times a day does he (kōm) _____ his hair?
13. I received a (sampl) _____ of soap powder in the mail.
14. She is training to be a (bämər) _____ pilot in the Air Force.
15. Instead of signing his real name, he chose to use a (sōōdənim) _____.

EXERCISES FOR REVIEW

A. Complete the spelling of the word whose definition is given in parentheses.

1. Could you please direct me to the lib_____y (place for books)?
2. We're going to march in the Vet_____ns (former soldiers) Day Parade.
3. What was his w_____t (number of pounds) before he started to diet?
4. Inci_____ly (By the way), I have to go on a diet too.
5. Unfortunately I don't find veg_____s (plant products used as food) pre_____ (to be chosen instead of) to desserts.
6. I believe I am na_____ly (by nature) meant to be pleasingly plump.
7. Jack is pract_____ly (almost completely) living at my house.
8. Your little dog is misch_____ous (playful).
9. We can't use the fireplace because the chim_____ (passage for smoke) is blocked.
10. Those students are very talented mus_____ly (in regard to music).

B. Complete the spelling of the words whose definitions are given in parentheses.

1. The entrance is thr_____ (by way of) the garden.
   Laura thr_____ (tossed) the ball.
2. Please si_____ (write your name) the check.
   Use the dotted li_____ (space to write on) at the bottom.
3. Would you shr_____k (scream loudly) if you saw a ghost?
   Let's play hide and s_____k (look-for game) with the children.
4. Wool feels r_____ (harsh) on my skin.
   Have the tailor fix the c_____ (turned-up fold) of this sleeve.

5. She's bringing the contract in her port_____olio (carrying case for papers).
   Give the prescription to the _____armacist (druggist).
6. Did you hear the horse n_____ (sound horse makes)?
   The vote was three ayes and one n_____ (no).
7. Did you br_____ (destroy) the vase?
   No wonder I have a head_____ (hurt).
8. When you dig weeds, be sure to get out the r_____t (part of the plant under the ground).
   I need a new s_____t (matching jacket and pants or skirt).
9. Before you go to sleep, please turn out the l_____t (illumination).
   That hill is the s_____te (location) for our new house.

C. Do you know how to play "Hot Pot"? This is a word game in which a definition calls for an answer that must have two words with the same sound. Thus, the definition "very warm cooking container" should bring the answer "hot pot." In the following, some letters are given to you as an extra clue.

1. tall structure made of cake ingredient   f_____r   t_____r
2. tossed into   thr_____   thr_____
3. harsh and resistant material   t_____   st_____
4. chart for measuring chuckles   l_____   gr_____
5. the one that was looked for was captured   s_____t   c_____t
6. a fearsome-looking location   fr_____t   s_____
7. to stitch, nevertheless   s_____,   th_____
8. a tardy baseball team missing one player   l_____   e_____t
9. grab the bends in legs   s_____   kn_____
10. a tidy piece of paper given after shopping   n_____t   re_____t

D. In the space provided correctly spell the word that is defined and given phonetically.

1. (nōm) _____ ugly little person
2. (nälij) _____ wisdom
3. (noomōnyə) _____ serious illness
4. (tōmān) _____ food poisoning
5. (fīt) _____ battle
6. (sent) _____ odor
7. (gōt) _____ barnyard animal
8. (lepərd) _____ jungle beast
9. (chôk) _____ used on blackboards
10. (floot) _____ musical instrument
11. (nē) _____ bendable part of leg
12. (zōn) _____ area, place
13. (luk) _____ fortune
14. (yōk) _____ egg yellow

9. HOMONYMS

Homonyms are words that sound alike but whose spelling and meaning are different. When is it *rode* and when *rowed* or *road?* Can you *pare* a *pair* of *pears?* Some people find it *too* hard *to* write out *"two."*

As these examples indicate, homonyms *must* be spelled correctly in order for their meaning to be understood. In this chapter you will:

1. learn how to distinguish between the most commonly confused homonyms
2. become familiar with a reference list of homonyms

THE MOST COMMONLY CONFUSED WORDS

The four groups of homonyms below are among the most commonly used and confused words in the English language. As you study them, remember that any misspelling will completely change the meaning you intend, and often make your sentence meaningless.

it's: contraction of *it is* *It's* time for breakfast.
its: possessive pronoun The dog caught *its* own tail.

you're: contraction of *you are* *You're* next.
your: possessive pronoun It is *your* turn.

they're: contraction of *they are* *They're* going to help me.
their: possessive pronoun They want you to return *their* books.

there: in that place Put it *there.*
      interjection *There,* that's done.
      impersonal construction *There* are three women here.

two: number Give me *two* hats.
to: direction Let's go *to* the store.
    part of infinitive I want *to* see the book.
too: also She *too* wanted the book.
    excessively It's *too* hot.

EXERCISE 1: Circle the appropriate word in each of the following sentences.

1. (It's/Its) strictly a matter of opinion.
2. The dog was guarding (its/it's) master's property.
3. Now (it's/its) time for us to leave.
4. The doll lost most of (it's/its) hair.
5. Where are (you're/your) shoes?
6. She said (you're/your) serious, but I think (you're/your) not.
7. Let's go back to (you're/your) house.
8. (You're/Your) taller than I am.
9. Put (their/they're/there) coats over (their/they're/there) on the couch.
10. Is (their/they're/there) anything I can do?
11. Stop arguing and put the flowers (their/they're/there).
12. They all said (their/they're/there) not going to do it.
13. All the artists put (their/they're/there) names on the paintings.
14. Ben went (to/too/two) the movies.
15. Sharon wanted to go (to/too/two).
16. Unfortunately, he didn't have (to/too/two) tickets.
17. Walking to school takes (to/too/two) much time.
18. May I have (to/too/two) pies for Jack (to/too/two) take (to/too/two) the fair, or do you want to carry food (to/too/two)?

A REFERENCE LIST OF COMMONLY USED HOMONYMS

In each of the following groups, the words are pronounced alike, or nearly alike—but the meanings and spellings differ. Context should give you clues to meanings. Misspellings will make a sentence meaningless.

> She gave her ascent to his proposal.

or hilarious:

The elegantly gowned bride was escorted down the isle by her father.

Although the list is long, your experience and common sense will already have taught you many of these homonyms. Study those that are not familiar to you, and try them out in sentences of your own. Then do the exercises that follow the Reference List of Homonyms.

aisle: passageway	The usher led us down the theater *aisle*.
isle: island	The boat landed on a deserted *isle*.
allowed: permitted	Tourists are not *allowed* inside the shrine.
aloud: spoken with a normal voice	I'll read *aloud* to the children.
all ready: everyone prepared	Are you *all ready*?
already: at or before this time	Have they *already* gone?
altar: a raised structure for worship	Put the flowers in front of the *altar*.
alter: change	We may have to *alter* our plans.
arc: curved line	The frisbee flew through the air in a long *arc*.
ark: large vessel	Noah filled his *ark* with many animals.
ascent: going up; slope	We'll start the *ascent* up the mountain tomorrow.
assent: agree	Did everyone in the group *assent* to the plan?
band: something that ties together	Put a *band* around those cartons.
group of people joined for common purpose; group of musicians	That *band* of people demonstrated yesterday.
banned: forbidden	Years ago that book was *banned*.

bare: uncovered	I'm the one with the *bare*, bald head.
bear: support, sustain the burden large heavy mammal	Please try to *bear* with me. Did you know that the teddy *bear* was named for Theodore Roosevelt?
base: bottom	See the rock at the *base* of the tree?
bass: lowest in music	Roger will sing the *bass* solo.
beach: sandy shore	Let's eat lunch at the *beach*.
beech: a kind of tree	The *beech* is a shade tree.
beat: defeat hit repeatedly	If I practice, I'll *beat* him. The traditional way to clean rugs was to *beat* them.
beet: vegetable	Sandra likes *beet* soup.
beau: admirer	My latest *beau* is strong and dumb.
bow: curve; knot	He wears a *bow* tie.
berry: small fruit	Try one *berry*.
bury: cover up	Let's *bury* our differences.
berth: sleeping place	Did you ever sleep in a *berth* in a railroad car?
birth: act of having offspring	Most women today go to a hospital for the *birth* of a child.
blew: past tense of *blow*	The wind *blew* the tree down.
blue: color	He bought a *blue* tie.
boar: male swine	A wild *boar* is bigger than a domestic pig.
bore: make a hole weary by being dull	*Bore* a hole for this hook. That film was a total *bore*.
born: brought into life	A calf was *born* this morning.
borne: past participle of *bear*	She has *borne* her trouble with dignity.
bough: branch	Trim the *bough* from this tree.
bow: bend	*Bow* your head.
brake: slow down	*Brake* at the stop sign.
break: shatter	*Break* the eggs into the bowl.
bread: food made of flour	Homemade *bread* is the best.
bred: past tense of *breed*	We *bred* German shepherds.

bridal: of a bride; of a wedding	Her *bridal* gown was handmade.
bridle: head harness for guiding a horse	Some Indians made *bridles* that were truly works of art.
to take offense	Naturally, I *bridled* at the insult.
by: preposition	*By* that time it will be too late
buy: to purchase	I like to *buy* things that are on sale.
canvas: coarse cloth	The *canvas* tent leaked.
canvass: examine; go through places or among people	The market research team *canvassed* the shoppers.
capital: most important, first-rate chief city or town money used in business	You have a *capital* idea. Our class visited the state *capital*. When we get enough *capital* we'll open a shoe store.
Capitol: building in which U.S. Congress meets; building in which state legislature meets	We're going to the *Capitol* today.
carat: unit of weight	The diamond weighed two *carats*.
carrot: vegetable	Do you like creamed *carrots*?
cede: give up title or one's rights	The loser had to *cede* his property.
seed: embryo	Plant the flower *seeds* near the fence.
cellar: room under a building	The furnace is in the *cellar*.
seller: one who sells	Who is the *seller* of that fine horse?
cent: small coin	Nothing costs only one *cent* any more.
scent: odor	I don't like the *scent* of tobacco.
sent: did send	They *sent* a sample.
cite: to quote; to refer to or mention as an example or proof	The lawyer will *cite* a previous case.
sight: view	It was a wonderful *sight*.
site: place	This is the perfect *site* for a picnic.
climb: mount, walk up	Can we *climb* this mountain today?
clime: climate	I refuse to hike uphill in this *clime!*

coarse: rough	The *coarse* cloth of this jacket hurts my neck.
course: path	The *course* of the marathon was changed.
class or lecture series	That *course* was filled so I had to sign up for another.
to run or move swiftly	The spring floods *course* over the rocks to form little waterfalls.
colonel: military officer	Does the *colonel* agree with me?
kernel: grain or seed of corn or other grain	To make corn pudding you must scrape the *kernels* off the cob.
complement: something added to complete a whole	Butter is the perfect *complement* to corn.
compliment: something said in admiration, praise or flattery	My *compliments* to the chef.
council: group of people called together for discussion, advice, government	The governor's advisory *council* meets next Wednesday.
counsel: advice	Helpful *counsel* often falls on deaf ears.
core: central part	There's a worm in the *core* of this apple.
corps: body of troops	He is a member of the Marine *Corps*.
creak: squeak	Did you hear the step *creak*?
creek: small stream	We can bathe in the *creek*.
dear: beloved, highly thought of	This ring is *dear* to me.
deer: wild animal	*Deer* hunting is not permitted here.
desert: abandon	I won't *desert* you.
dessert: last course of dinner	Cheese and crackers for *dessert*!
dew: moisture from air	The *dew* settled on the porch.
do: perform	Let's *do* it!
due: owed	The car payment is *due* today.
die: lose one's life	The prisoner will *die* in front of the firing squad.
dye: color	Let's *dye* the shirts green.

doe: female deer	The *doe* and her fawn passed our car.
dough: batter mixed for bread or cake	The baker kneaded the *dough*.
money (slang)	I've got to earn some *dough*.
dual: of two; double	The driver training car had *dual* steering wheels.
duel: fight between two	As you can imagine, driving that car became a *duel!*
faint: weak to pass out	We heard a *faint* call for help. He *fainted* whenever he saw blood.
feint: false show; pretended blow or attack to take opponent off guard	A *feint* with his right was followed by a smashing blow with his left.
find: discover **fined:** penalized	Did you *find* the hockey sticks? Every player was *fined*.
fair: attractive; clear **fare:** passage money	The forecast is cold and *fair*. The driver collected my bus *fare*.
fir: tree	We walked through a forest of *firs*.
fur: hair of animals	My *fur* collar is raccoon.
flea: small insect **flee:** run away	Have you ever seen a *flea* circus? The captive wanted to *flee*.
flew: past tense of *fly* **flue:** pipe or passage for smoke, as in a chimney	We *flew* to California. He got to the roof through the *flue*.
flour: ground meal	I make bread with whole wheat *flour*.
flower: blossom	Here's a vase for the *flowers*.
for: preposition **fore:** in or at the front **four:** two plus two	Would you please do it *for* me? Her talents came to the *fore*. I need *four* spoons.
forth: out **fourth:** next after third	The leader urged us to go *forth*. It rained on the *fourth* day of our stay.
foul: impure **fowl:** bird	The *foul* air made him sick. A hen is a *fowl*.

gait: manner of walking or running **gate:** entrance	After the accident she walked with a halting *gait*. Walk through the *gate* and turn left.
gilt: covered with gold **guilt:** being at fault	I bought a mirror with a *gilt* edge. Her blushes showed her sense of *guilt*.
gorilla: large ape **guerrilla:** irregular soldier, usually a revolutionary	There are quite a few *gorillas* in the Bronx Zoo. The *guerrillas* dynamited the train.
grate: fireplace **great:** important large	He built a fire in the *grate*. Gandhi was a *great* man. The nation's deficit is *greater* than ever.
groan: moan **grown:** past participle of *grow*	Mark *groaned* when he failed the test. My! How tall you've *grown!*
guessed: past tense of guess **guest:** visitor	Have you *guessed* the answer? Sara is the *guest* of honor.
hail: ice particles call out or greet **hale:** strong	The *hail* hit against the windows. The victorious troops were *hailed* on their return. He has been *hale* and hearty all his life.
hair: a filament **hare:** a rabbit-like animal	He is losing his *hair*. *Hares* are raised on this farm.
hall: passageway **haul:** pull	Meet me in the *hall*. *Haul* in the nets.
hart: a stag **heart:** core body organ that circulates blood	The wounded *hart* fell to the ground. Get to the *heart* of the matter. She has a weak *heart*.
heal: cure **heel:** back of foot cad, an unscrupulous person	How long will it take for the wound to *heal?* The shoe rubbed against his *heel*. His reputation as a *heel* was well deserved.

hear: listen	Can you *hear* the bells?
here: in this place	Put the package *here*.
heard: past tense of *hear*	Have you *heard* the news?
herd: group	The *herd* of goats is blocking the road.
him: objective case of the pronoun *he*	Let's hire *him*.
hymn: sacred song	I mean the man who's singing the *hymn*.
hoarse: having a rough voice	She sang until she was *hoarse*.
horse: animal	I board my *horse* in that stable.
hole: cavity	The *hole* is filling up with water.
whole: entire	I am telling you the *whole* truth.
holy: sacred	Don't photograph the *holy* shrine.
wholly: entirely	You are *wholly* right in your claim.
hour: sixty minutes	The train is an *hour* late.
our: belonging to us	Now it's *our* turn.
idle: inactive	The *idle* man needs a job.
idol: image for worship	Let's ask him to polish the *idol*.
in: within	It is *in* the special room.
inn: establishment providing food, drink, lodging for travelers	The special room is at the *inn*.
incite: stir up	Do you think he can be *incited* to work?
insight: understanding	We must help him gain the necessary *insight*.
knew: past tense of *know*	I *knew* he would like that present.
new: not old	He needed a *new* watch.
knight: one with title of Sir	The *knight* tripped over his armor.
night: sunset to sunrise	He tripped because he couldn't see at *night*.
know: understand	He didn't *know* anything about electricity.
no: negative	*No*, that is not true.
lain: past participle of *lie*	The idle man has *lain* there all day.
lane: narrow road	He lives on Cherry *Lane*.

lead: metal	The *lead* soldiers are in the box.
led: past tense of *lead*	The firefighters *led* us to safety.
lessen: grow smaller	Our fear *lessened* when the police arrived.
lesson: pupil's task	My piano *lesson* went very well.
lie: recline a false statement **lye:** strong alkaline substance	*Lie* on the couch and rest. You must not tell a *lie*. The *lye* burned my hand.
load: burden **lode:** vein of metallic ore	I can't carry that *load* alone. The *lode* was rich in gold.
loan: thing lent **lone:** single	The payment on the *loan* is due. Texas is called the *Lone* Star State.
made: past tense of *make* **maid:** young woman or female servant	She *made* her own clothes. The *maid* works five days a week.
mail: letters **male:** masculine; man	Pick up the *mail* at the post office. That used to be a club for *males* only.
main: chief **mane:** long hair on neck of animals	What is the *main* reason you study? The groom brushed the horse's *mane*.
meat: flesh **meet:** come together	I only eat *meat* once a week. Let's *meet* at noon.
metal: mineral **mettle:** courage	The posts are made of *metal*. This task will test your *mettle*.
miner: one who digs underground **minor:** one who is underage inferior; not serious	My friend in West Virginia is a *miner*. Liquor cannot be served to a *minor*. She suffered a *minor* injury.
morn: morning **mourn:** grieve	A spring *morn* always lifts my spirits. He *mourned* the death of his friend.
one: a single unit **won:** past tense of *win*	*One* worry at a time is enough. He *won* the scholarship this year.

pail: vessel for liquids	He dropped the *pail* of milk.
pale: colorless	The once ruddy man had turned quite *pale*.
pain: distress	Edward winced with *pain*.
pane: sheet of glass	The *pane* of glass was shattered.
pair: couple	She bought a *pair* of bookcases.
pare: shave off	*Pare* the apples for the pie.
pear: fruit	Would you like a stewed *pear*?
passed: past tense of *pass*	We *passed* on the street.
past: time gone by	The *past* year has been difficult for us.
peal: loud sound	We heard *peals* of laughter at the show.
peel: skin of fruit	Watch out for that banana *peel*.
plain: clear; obvious	His words were *plain* to all of us.
not luxurious; not good-looking	She wore a *plain* blouse.
plane: flat, level surface	The *plane* was treeless.
a carpenter's tool	Borrow my *plane* to smooth the tabletop.
short for *airplane*	The *plane* had to circle for hours before we could land.
pore: to read or study carefully	She *pored* over the latest science fiction novel.
tiny opening in plant leaf or skin	He perspired from every *pore* in his body.
pour: to flow or cause to flow	Will you *pour* the tea?
pray: beseech	We *prayed* for her recovery.
prey: plunder; hunt; make a profit from a victim	He *preyed* upon people who were weak.
victim	The leopard stalked its *prey*.
principal: head of school	Who is the new high school *principal*?
chief; main	What is the *principal* problem of society today?
principle: fundamental rule or truth	The editorial discussed the *principle* of religious freedom.
profit: gain	The company's *profit* was down this year.
prophet: one who foretells	It is a book about a *prophet's* life.

rain: shower	Don't you wish it would *rain* money?
reign: rule	Queen Victoria *reigned* for many years.
rein: part of a harness	The *reins* snapped when the horse ran away.
rap: knock	The chairman should *rap* the gavel for quiet.
wrap: fold a covering around	*Wrap* the gift in blue paper.
read: understand written words	*Read* at least one newspaper every day.
reed: hollow stalk	Tall *reeds* grow along the riverbank.
read: past tense of *read*	I *read* the newspaper yesterday.
red: the color	Roses are not always *red*.
real: genuine	This is *real* ivory.
reel: spool	The fish took all the line off the *reel*.
right: proper	Giving back the money was the *right* thing to do.
opposite of left	Turn *right* at the corner.
rite: ceremony	The minister performed the marriage *rite*.
write: to draw letters and words on paper	Will you *write* to me while you are away?
ring: circle	The children formed a *ring* for their game.
wring: twist	*Wring* out your bathing suits.
road: highway	I'm looking for the *road* to fame and fortune.
rode: past tense of *ride*	He *rode* his bike all morning.
rowed: past tense of *row*	They *rowed* that boat yesterday.
role: part	She has the main *role* in the play.
roll: revolve	The locked wheels can't *roll*.
small bread	Pass me a *roll*.
root: origin	People say money is the *root* of all evil.
route: course	One *route* to success is hard work.
rote: memorizing by repetition	Pupils often learn the multiplication tables by *rote*.
wrote: past tense of *write*	He *wrote* a best-seller last year.

sail: navigate
sheet of material to catch or deflect the wind
sale: act of selling

We plan to *sail* to Florida.
The *sail* was torn.

That shop has a *sale* every month.

---

scene: division of a play

The first *scene* is the best.

seen: past participle of *see*

Have you *seen* the new play?

---

sea: ocean
see: observe

I used to live near the *sea*.
Did you *see* the new teacher dance?

---

seam: line of joining

seem: appear

His suit jacket split at the back *seam*.
The tailor *seems* to know her business.

---

sew: use needle and thread
so: very; in such a manner

sow: scatter, as with seed

Please *sew* that seam.
Repair it *so* the damage won't show.
Can we *sow* kindness as if it were beans?

---

slay: kill

sleigh: sled

If I had a dragon, would you *slay* it?
I gave Jack a *sleigh* for Christmas.

---

soar: fly high into the air

sore: painful

The red kite *soared* higher than the blue one.
Flying makes my arms *sore*.

---

sold: past tense of *sell*
soled: having a sole

She *sold* her plane to Fred.
You need to have your shoes *soled*.

---

sole: only

under part of a shoe
kind of fish

soul: spirit

You are the *sole* owner of those shoes.
There is a hole in the right *sole*.
I must buy some *sole* fillets for dinner.
Some people believe that animals other than humans have a *soul* too.

---

some: quantity

sum: whole amount

I wish I had *some* of your qualities.
The *sum* of my immediate profit is small.

son: male descendant	Unfortunately, my *son* took the whole sum.
sun: source of light	The *sun* was in my eyes so I didn't see him.
stake: post	Drive a *stake* into the vampire's heart!
steak: slice of meat	I like rare *steak*.
stare: gaze at	I *stare* when I see someone eating a rare steak.
stair: step	I climbed the *stairs* to get a better view.
stationary: fixed	The marble statue is *stationary*.
stationery: writing paper	I ordered new *stationery*.
steal: rob	Last night someone tried to *steal* the stationary statue.
steel: metal	They sawed through a *steel* door to get to it.
straight: direct	First they followed the *straight* path.
strait: narrow passage between bodies of water	Gibraltar overlooks an important *strait*.
suite: group of connected rooms	The company took a *suite* at the hotel.
sweet: sugary	This candy is much too *sweet*.
tail: part of an animal's body	The dog wagged its *tail*.
tale: story	This is a *tale* about a dog's tail.
team: set of players	I joined the tennis *team* yesterday.
teem: abound; to pour	Unfortunately we couldn't play because of the *teeming* rain.
threw: past tense of *throw*	Who *threw* the soggy ball at me?
through: from end to end	I saw the culprit *through* my telescope.
throne: chair of state	Where did you put my *throne*?
thrown: past participle of *throw*	It was *thrown* away.
tide: rise and fall of the ocean	Perhaps my throne will come in with the *tide*.
tied: past tense of *tie*	My crown was *tied* to the back of my throne.

toe: digit of the foot	I stubbed my *toe*.
tow: pull	The *tow* line pulled the raft.
told: past tense of *tell*	I *told* the lifeguard to take it easy.
tolled: past tense of *toll*	The bells *tolled* when we landed on the beach.
vain: useless	I ran in a *vain* attempt to catch you.
conceited	He was a *vain* man.
vane: flat piece of metal, or other material that shows which way the wind is blowing	There's a *vane* on the barn roof.
vein: streak; blood vessel	The blood in our *veins* is blue.
vale: valley	She lives in the *vale*.
veil: light fabric that covers the face	In this country women seldom wear a *veil* any more.
vial: small bottle	There is perfume in the *vial* on the table.
vile: repulsive	Unfortunately, the perfume is *vile*.
wade: walk through water	Don't *wade* with your shoes on.
weighed: past tense of *weigh*	If you do, they will be *weighed* down with water.
wail: lament	A *wail* went up when he dropped the ball.
whale: large water-dwelling mammal	The fullback who hit him was as powerful as a *whale*.
waist: middle part of body	He grabbed him around the *waist*.
waste: loss	That game was a big *waste* of time.
wait: remain	No one wanted to *wait* to see what would happen.
weight: heaviness	We all felt the *weight* of the loss.
wares: articles for sale	The street vendor spread out his *wares*.
wears: becomes used	The heels of his shoes began to *wear*.
to have on the body	He *wears* the things he cannot sell.

Homonyms / 117

way: road or path	We went on our *way* after we saw you.
course of action	Is that the correct *way* to type?
weigh: to figure the heaviness of something	Use the scale to *weigh* yourself.
weak: feeble	I made a *weak* effort to resist his sales pitch.
week: seven days	I make this effort every *week*.
weather: atmospheric conditions	The rainy *weather* helped me.
whether: in case, if	But he's usually there *whether* it's sunny or not.
which: pronoun	*Which* shirt shall I buy?
witch: sorceress	When I grow up, I want to be a *witch*.
whine: complain	I will turn people who *whine* into toads.
wine: fermented grape juice	Then I will celebrate with a glass of good *wine*.
wood: timber	I will keep the toads in a cage made of *wood*.
would: past tense of *will*	*Would* you please watch those toads for me?

EXERCISE 2: Select the correct word from each pair in parentheses. You can find all of these homonym sets in the preceding list. When you are finished, check your answers. Go back to the list and mark any homonyms that are giving you trouble so you can study them further.

My very (deer/dear) friend:

I believe we haven't (scene/seen) each other since that (knight/night) the (band/banned) played for us in the (seller/cellar) of your house on the (isle/aisle). We were (so/sew/sow) close as you (rode/road/rowed) across the little lake. Ah, do you remember the (cite/site/sight) of the moonlight on the (beach/beech) when we landed? You said you would (dew/do/due) anything I wanted: (peel/peal) a bunch of grapes, (clime/climb) the highest mountain, fight a (duel/dual), (sale/sail) a yacht across the (sea/see), even buy me my own (plane/plain). You paid me so many (compliments/complements). In the (mourn/morn) I had to (write/rite/right) them down in my most (wholly/holy) book—my diary. I chose a beautiful (flour/flower) to mark the page I love most and which I often (reed/read) (allowed/aloud).

I don't want to (boar/bore) you any longer so I will tell you what happened after I (through/threw) you out. I had a sudden (insight/incite). Sorry to say, my (suite/sweet), I (find/fined) you really are an awful (pain/pane). Anyway, I can not (ascent/assent) to your offer of marriage, because it would (altar/alter) my life style (to/too/two) much. I decided to change (course/coarse) and go after some (dough/doe). So (hear/here) is my (grate/great) news: I AM GOING TO BE A MUD WRESTLER!

EXERCISE 3: There is an error in every sentence below. Find and correct it.

1. The nervous player hit three fowl balls.
2. Did he break the car in time?
3. Surely she didn't eat the hole cake!
4. Her gilt was written all over her face.
5. Is that pot made of mettle that conducts heat well?
6. The sailors had to hall in the anchor.
7. Flea for your lives!
8. His hart was broken when she left him.
9. But I maid the bed yesterday.
10. Let's teem up together.
11. Don't stair!
12. You must do it weather you want to or not.
13. Please pass the carats.

14. We'll be an our late.
15. Jack and Jill are always carrying that pale of water.
16. Whose turn is it to pore the lemonade?

AND SOME NEAR-HOMONYMS

The words in each of the following pairs are easy to confuse because their pronunciations—and spellings—are similar. These words are pronounced differently enough, though, that they are not quite homonyms. Correct pronunciation is a step toward correct spelling. In some cases, the pronunciation depends on the syllable that is stressed. In others, clearly pronouncing a prefix or a final letter can make all the difference.

accept: receive	Please *accept* this gift.
except: exclude	Everyone has brought a gift *except* Bill.
addition: increase; joining of one thing to another	This book is in *addition* to my other gift.
edition: copies printed at one time	It's a first *edition* of a Faulkner novel.
affect: to influence or alter	Reading it will *affect* your view of his talent.
effect: result	That is certainly the *effect* it had on me.
to cause or bring about	Do you think a new President can really *effect* change?
allusion: reference	Don't make any *allusions* to his second head.
illusion: deceptive	It happens to be real, not an *illusion*.
assistance: help	May I have your *assistance*?
assistants: those who help	Jack's *assistants* are ignoring me.
deceased: dead	The memorial service is for *deceased* soldiers.
diseased: ill	The *diseased* horses were treated by the veterinarian.

envelop: wrap up, cover	This fog will *envelop* the mountain by noon.
envelope: folded paper container for letters	This *envelope* has your name on it.
formally: in a formal manner	We were *formally* introduced.
formerly: at one time	*Formerly* we were neighbors.
higher: more elevated	The mountain climbers went *higher*.
hire: to pay for services or things	They *hired* a guide to lead them to the top of Mount Everest.
loose: free; not firmly fastened down	Jenny's *loose* tooth came out when she sneezed.
lose: mislay; suffer loss; be deprived of	She put the tooth in her pocket so she wouldn't *lose* it.
moral: ethical issue	What is the *moral* of the story?
morale: mental state	Think what that would do to her *morale!*
of: preposition; derived from; resulting from; caused by; about	She died *of* cancer.
off: keep away; no longer attached; no longer in operation	The plane takes *off* in five minutes.
personal: private, individual	Please write *"personal"* on the envelope.
personnel: employees	I don't want all the office *personnel* to read it.
picture: graphic representation	That *picture* of me is wonderful!
pitcher: vessel for liquids	Fill up the pitcher and we'll drink all day.
baseball player who throws balls (pitches) to the batters	The *pitcher* threw so many balls he was taken out of the game.
prophecy: prediction	Do you believe the *prophecy* about interest rates?
prophesy: to foretell	Who can *prophesy* what the economy will do next year?
stable: firm, steady	Fix that leg so the table will be *stable*.
building for horses or cattle	How is a *stable* different from a barn?
staple: thin wire that binds things together; also, to attach things with such a wire	*Staple* the pages together.

statue: form of person or animal in stone, wood, etc.	Put the *statue* in the garden.
stature: height of person in standing position	He has the *stature* of a pole vaulter.
statute: law	The new tax *statute* was passed by Congress.
suit: outfit	That *suit* is for the wedding.
suite: connecting rooms	We can dress in the *suite* upstairs.
than: used to make a comparison	We don't want to be any later *than* the other guests.
then: at that time	We'll be able to talk to everybody *then*.
trail: path	The *trail* led between the trees.
trial: court hearing	Type the testimony from the *trial*.
were: plural of *was*	The men *were* ready to work at eight.
where: at what place	*Where* can you find a repair shop?
woman: one female	That *woman* was hired because her skills were outstanding.
women: plural of *woman*	The other *women* were disappointed because they did not get a chance to try out for the job.

EXERCISE 4: Circle the correct word from each pair in parentheses.

There is a problem in this office and it is (affecting/effecting) everyone's (morale/moral). The man who works as an (assistance/assistant) to the vice president for human resources thinks that if he stays (were/where) he is supposed to be—at his desk planning the (addition/edition) of a new computer system—he will be promoted to vice president of the company. What an (allusion/illusion)!

At first he looked like a (stature/statue). Some of the (woman/women) thought he must be (deceased/diseased) when he came to work with us. He seemed stranger (then/than) anyone else in the office.

That man is not a (personal/personnel) expert. (Formerly/Formally) he was a (picture/pitcher) for a baseball team. No wonder he tends to (loose/lose) copies (of/off) important papers. Also, he never puts papers in the right (envelop/envelope). He is not a (staple/stable) individual. It is a (trail/trial) to work in the same (suit/suite) with him.

My (prohecy/prophesy) is that he will not go any (hire/higher) in this company. Besides, I can't see anyone in the job of vice president (accept/except) me!

EXERCISE 5: In each paragraph below, choose the correct word from the pair of words in parentheses.

1. The men who (were/where) at the (scene/seen) of the accident (would/wood) later (write/rite) that the (rain/rein), which had been falling (for/four) (hours/ours), was the (principle/principal) cause. The troopers (blew/blue) (there/their) whistles, but the driver (passed/past) (so/sew) close the car could not avoid the (whole/hole) in the (rode/road). Of (coarse/course) they all (new/knew) the (whether/weather) was bad.

2. When the (son/sun) glares (threw/through) the trees, automobiles kill many (deer/dear) as the animals run back and (forth/fourth) across (sum/some) of our most-traveled (roots/routes). The drivers can't (see/sea) clearly, and they (seam/seem) to have trouble (braking/breaking) in time. The (deceased/diseased) animals have to be (toed/towed) away. Later we must (berry/bury) them. What a (waist/waste) of such lovely creatures!

3. (Their/They're) letter will (knot/not) be (sent/scent) by the (to/two) o'clock (mail/male) unless you (by/buy) another twenty-(cent/scent) stamp. Extra postage is (do/due) since (it's/its) (weight/wait) is (grater/greater) (than/then) (one/won) ounce. If (there/they're) is (to/too) little postage, the post office won't (accept/except) the (envelop/envelope).

4. I (wrote/rote) a book about the (see/sea) which explained the (right/rite) (way/weight) to (sale/sail) to Italy. I shall (altar/alter) (some/sum) parts of it later if I am (aloud/allowed) to (by/buy) the publisher. (Then/Than) I will (higher/hire) someone from the (personal/personnel) department to work on it. I don't expect to make a (prophet/profit) on it, but I (do/dew) hope it will be (read/red). If anyone should (fined/find) a mistake, I can always fix it in the second (addition/edition).

EXERCISES FOR REVIEW

A. Circle the correct form of the words in parentheses in each of the following sentences.

1. I (to/too) will need more time to finish.
2. He told me that (their/they're) nearing the objective.
3. The work was much (to/too) difficult to finish in one day.
4. Will you let Edna know if (you're/your) going to the party?
5. Will you please give them (there/their) notebooks.
6. The hat lost (its/it's) shape in the rain.
7. Put the packages on the desk over (there/their).
8. You will have to pay at least (too/two) dollars for the cake.
9. (You're/Your) just the person I have been looking for.
10. (Its/It's) time to leave for the airport.
11. They must learn to do (there/their) own research work.
12. (There/They're) not going to like this!

13. They spoke (to/too) rapidly for me to understand.
14. The puppy whined for (its/it's) mother.
15. Have you seen (their/there) latest model?
16. Will you give me (you're/your) promise now?

B. One sentence in each of the following groups is correct, and the other sentence contains an error. Correct the errors.

1. (a) Sparks flue up the chimney.
   (b) The idle worker watched the foreman work.
2. (a) She shouted so long her voice is horse.
   (b) Who built the model of the ark?
3. (a) What is the fare from Dublin to New York City?
   (b) I ate too much desert.
4. (a) Give me the forth cake.
   (b) She walked through the gate.
5. (a) I never would have guest the truth.
   (b) Just give me the bare facts.
6. (a) Have you learned your lessen?
   (b) That man looks hale and hearty to me.
7. (a) One man's meet is another man's poison.
   (b) When was the mail delivered?
8. (a) My principle reason is that they need our help.
   (b) The principal of the school is an old friend.
9. (a) The referee blew his whistle.
   (b) The reign had been falling for hours.
10. (a) Naturally they new their way around the city.
    (b) They had all been bred to urban life.
11. (a) We had to order new stationery when the company's name was changed.
    (b) Our wears are selling quite well this year.

12. (a) Her bridle gown had yards and yards of lace.

(b) They had to take out a loan to pay for their new car.

13. (a) They made a handsome pare at the ceremony.

(b) Have you ever eaten a berry that was freshly picked?

14. (a) Did you have to sleep in the upper berth on your cruise?

(b) It seams uncomfortable to me.

15. (a) We past them right by.

(b) Which computer did they choose?

16. (a) I'll follow them after the son sets.

(b) I want to hear the new bass at the opera.

17. (a) When did you buy it?

(b) Did you get it gift wrapped with a beau tied around the box?

C. Choose the correct word from each pair in parentheses.

As Juan drove down the (lain/lane) he was sure the (counsel/council) members (would/wood) (no/know) they should follow. He went along (one/won) of the (capital's/Capitol's) most scenic (roots/routes). The (kernel/colonel) was supposed to be in the car, but he hadn't been (herd/heard) from in a (weak/week). They (rote/wrote) a memo and (cent/sent) it by (male/mail). Juan had learned that he was (already/all ready) to lead a new (core/corps) of troops. Perhaps he was staying at the (in/inn) on the other side of the (creek/creak). Our opponents will (beat/beet) (hymn/him) in the next election (four/for) sure, Juan thought, as he drove (strait/straight) into a (toe/tow) truck. Fortunately a (fur/fir) tree stood in the (way/weigh) of the car, and its (bows/boughs) cushioned the blow. As Juan (told/tolled) the story, only his (waste/waist) was (sore/soar). "I never (lye/lie)," thought Juan with a (grown/groan). Although he felt (feint/faint) he was not prepared to (cede/seed) the election.

"I've (born/borne) heavy (lodes/loads) before," he said. "There's no (prophet/profit) in losing. I'll (canvas/canvass) the district myself. I'll (wrap/rap) on every door and (ring/wring) every bell. I'll even (prey/pray). My (heels/heals) and (souls/soles) will ache, but a dinner of (stake/steak) and (whine/wine) should revive me. I have (lead/led) many campaigns before. The opposition's efforts will be in (vein/vain). They are (vial/vile), bringing in (gorillas/guerrillas) who hide by day and (sleigh/slay) by night. Most of them are too young to (dye/die), too—they're still (minors/miners) and so they can't even vote. Their (main/mane) interest is making (some/sum) money, and when we catch them they run like (hairs/hares). They (steel/steal) and then they (wail/whale). Did that party dream that we would let the (thrown/throne) be (soled/sold)? But now I must (weighed/wade) into the (veil/vale) below in order to catch up with the others. I'm lucky the (tide/tied) is low. Will I have a (tail/tale) to tell them! We all have a (roll/role) to play in this (reel/real)-life drama."

D. Circle the correct word from each pair in parentheses in each of the paragraphs below.

1. The pace on the mountain (trail/trial) was faster (then/than) we had thought. The (woman/women) who had been ill needed some (assistance/assistants) in order to keep up. We feared she would (loose/lose) the way. But her (moral/morale) was (hire/higher) at the end of the hike. From the top (of/off) the hill we watched the mist (envelop/envelope) the lake below. The (picture/pitcher) was so lovely it was hard to believe it was not an (allusion/illusion).

2. I have decided to go (were/where) no one has ever been before. Last month the Exploration Society (accepted/excepted) me as a member. I was (formally/formerly) inducted in a ceremony held in a (stable/staple). It had been built as an (addition/edition) to a farmhouse. It was beautifully designed, with (statures/statues) lining the driveway. The ceremonies began with a memorial to all (deceased/diseased) members. I wore a (suite/suit) for the occasion. I don't mind taking (personal/personnel) risks, and I gladly (prophecy/prophesy) that I will achieve my goal: to (affect/effect) a complete change in my life.

E. There is an error in every sentence below. Find each error and write the correct word.

1. Too dollars is a bargain price for a movie.
2. I've scene that one before.
3. Did you see the pitcher that got all the Academy Awards?
4. I've been there all ready.
5. Their going tomorrow.
6. Its got marvelous photography.
7. I like adventure films better then comedies.
8. Imagine, a guerrilla wearing a person suit!
9. Jane said she never would have guest who the real beast was.
10. If we hurry we can see it before it's band.
11. I bet I can beet you to the bus stop!
12. Do you have enough money for the bus fair?
13. I would accept that I spent some this morning.
14. My shoes needed new souls.
15. I had to complement the shoemaker.
16. She was wearing an attractive suite.
17. It was an unusual shade of blew.
18. Her perfume had a lovely cent, too.

19. I only went inn for a minute.
20. Her conversation was sew interesting, though.
21. I found I had been there for an our.
22. Formally, I would never had talked so long.
23. At knight I'm going to check out all my shoes.
24. I want to get them repaired next weak.
25. I'd better get a staple job so I can take her out for dinner.

10. CAPITALIZATION

> did you see the two holes in the head last tuesday or were you too busy shooting scarface and the little angels at the empire state building?

This question is written in plain English, but it is difficult to understand because it has no capital letters.

> Did you see *The Two Holes in the Head* last Tuesday or were you too busy shooting *Scarface and the Little Angels* at the Empire State Building?

Now the above sentence makes sense. The capital letters help the reader to extract the meaning.

In this chapter you will learn when to use capital letters for:

1. first words
2. particular people
3. particular places
4. particular things
5. times and events

As you saw in the example that started this chapter, capitalization can change the way we interpret what we read. For this reason it is considered an adjunct of spelling. This chapter deals with the uses of capitalization that you are most likely to come across. For a more detailed discussion of the subject, and for additions or exceptions to the rules given here, you may want to consult a grammar or usage test or a good dictionary.

RULES FOR FIRSTS

Sentences and Quotations

RULE 1: Capitalize the first word of a sentence.

>   Go to the beach.   Do not park here.

RULE 2: Capitalize the first word in a direct quotation.

Jaime said, "Leave the keys on the table."
"Leave the keys," Jaime said. "There are no extra ones in the house."

BUT

"If you leave the keys," Jaime said, "put them on the table."

The word "put" is not capitalized because it does not begin a new sentence.

NOTE: Do not capitalize the first word of an *indirect* quotation.

Jaime said that we should put the keys on the table.

Titles and Poetry

RULE 3: Capitalize the first word, the last word and all the important words in the title of a book, a movie, a play, a song, an opera or any other type of composition. Important words are all words except prepositions and words such as *and, the, a,* and *or.*

    The Ballad of the Sad Cafe
    War and Peace
    I Dream of Jeannie with the Light Brown Hair
    The World I Lived In

RULE 4: Capitalize the first word of each line of poetry. However, if a line of poetry is continued on a second line, do not capitalize the first word of the part which runs over. A distinctive characteristic of many poets, though, is that they make their own rules about style, including capitalization, in their works. When you are copying a poem (or part of a poem), follow the poet's style exactly.

Letter-Writing

RULE 5: Capitalize the first word and all nouns in the salutation of a letter.

    Dear Bert,   Dear Sir:
    My dear Sir: My dear Mrs. Stewart,

Note that "dear" is an adjective, and therefore it is not capitalized.

RULE 6: Capitalize the first word of the complimentary close.

    Sincerely yours,   Cordially yours,
    Very truly yours,   With best wishes,

EXERCISE 1: Capitalize letters where needed. Add periods at the ends of sentences if necessary and quotation marks where they are needed.

who wants to see the play rotten bananas smell? Sam told me that he does not want to go. Robert said, "please leave two tickets for me," shall we meet at the theater? Sharon left this note for me:

dear linda,
    please order four tickets for the opening night of the opera false teeth feel funny
    thank you

                                                    with best wishes,
                                                          Sharon

RULES FOR PARTICULAR PEOPLE

The Deity

RULE 7: Capitalize all words denoting the Deity.

God	Allah	Jehovah	Supreme Being
Holy Ghost	Most High	the Word	Adonai

NOTE: Pronouns relating to the Deity are capitalized always when necessary to avoid ambiguity, and are often capitalized even when no ambiguity exists.

                        Trust in Him.

BUT

        God in his mercy   *or*   God in His mercy

Names and Titles

RULE 1: Capitalize the names of people and the adjectives derived from those names.

>Shakespeare—Shakespearean
>Jefferson—Jeffersonian

RULE 2: Capitalize titles when they are used as part of a person's name.

Aunt Ellen   Judge Dan Donaldson
Uncle George   Governor William Morris

BUT

>My aunt works for the union.
>The governor gives the State of the State Address.

The words "aunt" and "governor" are not capitalized because they are not used as part of a person's name.

NOTE: The word "President" is always capitalized when referring to the President of the United States.

>The President is preparing his State of the Union Address.

BUT

>The president of the auto company drove cross-country on vacation.

RULE 3: Capitalize titles when they are used in direct address.

>Can you join us for lunch, Professor?
>We have a few questions for you, Governor.

RULE 4: The words *Mother, Dad, Father* are capitalized when they are used in place of a person's name.

>Where is Mother?

BUT

>Where is my mother?

The word *mother* in the second sentence is not capitalized because it is not used in place of a name; it is used with the pronoun *my*.

RULE 5: Always capitalize the pronoun *I*.

Names of Groups

RULE 6: Capitalize the names of religions and religious groups, races, political parties, and the adjectives derived from them.

Catholics   Catholicism   Oriental
Democratic Party   Democrat

NOTE: When these words are used to have a more general meaning they are not capitalized.

The democratic way of life means more than simply voting every four years.

RULE 7: Capitalize the names of governmental groups and departments.

Security Council   House of Representatives
Senate   Department of Sanitation

NOTE: Do not capitalize general or incomplete names of government groups.

a city department
a national agency

EXERCISE 2: Add the necessary capital letters to the following. Also add periods at the end of sentences where necessary.

my dear angela,
    here's the latest news! our department is planning a farewell party for ed he's moving to the country to raise goats. we wanted to give him a book about goats from the department of agriculture but then mary said, "he probably has all the books he needs." i said that he did not. but you can't argue with mary! she is always praying and says the almighty tells her everything in her dreams. not even a supreme court decision could change her mind. did i tell you it is going to be a surprise party? the surprise is—we're giving ed a goat!
                                        with lots of love,

                                              brenda

EXERCISE 3: Capitalize where necessary.

1. emerson's writings
2. mexican hayride
3. republican form of government
4. united nations
5. roman countryside
6. general pershing
7. aunt carol
8. my grandfather
9. father adams
10. star wars
11. the star-spangled banner
12. to whom it may concern:
13. socratic
14. social democratic party

RULES FOR PLACES AND THINGS

Places (on Earth and Otherwise)

RULE 1: Capitalize the names of nations, states, cities, regions, streets, and buildings.

Ireland	Nebraska	the Deep South
Fifth Avenue	East Germany	Saskatchewan
Maple Street	Chrysler Building	North Plainfield
Moscow	Northwest Passage	Buckinghamshire

NOTE: the words *north, south, east, west* are capitalized when they are part of a name or when they refer to a region. They are not capitalized when they are used to show direction:

Sara drove north for ten miles.

RULE 2: Capitalize the names of stars, galaxies, constellations, and planets. Capitalize the words *sun, earth,* and *moon* only when they appear with the capitalized names of planets.

Sirius   Milky Way   Big Dipper

The astronauts on the space shuttle saw Mars.
We have space pictures of Saturn, the Moon, and the Earth.

BUT
>The earth is far from the sun.

The words *earth* and *sun* are not capitalized here because they are not listed with capitalized names of planets.

EXERCISE 4: Capitalize words when necessary in the following sentences.

1. Have you ever visited the statue of liberty in new york?
2. I think Hal lives south of park avenue.
3. My garden is on the east side of the house.
4. I'm planning a trip to north carolina next month.
5. Sometimes venus is referred to as the evening star.
6. The new england states will probably lose population in the next decade.
7. If you drive east for two miles you will hit south main street.
8. Have you ever seen the century building?
9. We will tour southeast asia next month.
10. Would you like to view mercury and the sun through the telescope?

Organizations

RULE 3: Capitalize the names of companies and organizations.
>Jack works for United Chair and Table Company.

BUT
>Jack works for a furniture manufacturing company.

The words "furniture manufacturing company" are not capitalized because they do not name a particular company.
>Pete used to play for the Yankees.

BUT
>Pete used to play for a baseball team.

The words "baseball team" are not capitalized because they do not name a particular organization.

RULE 4: Capitalize the names of schools, colleges, and institutions.

> My friend teaches at Indiana University.
> She interned at Memorial Hospital.
> Where is Pleasantville High School?

BUT

> Where is the high school?
> Do you go to college?

The words "high school" and "college" are not part of a name. Therefore they are not capitalized.

NOTE: Do not capitalize terms designating academic years.

> freshman   junior
> sophomore   senior

School Subjects and Printed Matter

RULE 5: Capitalize the names of languages and the names of school subjects derived from the names of languages.

> You can study English, Italian, and French in summer school.

BUT

> You cannot study mathematics or bookkeeping.

The subjects mathematics and bookkeeping are not derived from the names of languages so they are not capitalized.

RULE 6: Capitalize names of publications, trade names, and historical documents.

> Do you read the *Atlantic Monthly*?
> I just bought a Firebird.
> The Magna Carta is in the British Museum.
> Where is the copy of the Bill of Rights?

RULE 7: Capitalize acronyms and abbreviations of words if the words themselves are capitalized.

> James works for the A.S.P.C.A.

This abbreviation stands for American Society for the Prevention of Cruelty to Animals. Since the name is capitalized, the abbreviation for the name is also capitalized.

BUT

The national speed limit is 55 m.p.h.

Since "miles per hour" is not capitalized, the abbreviation is not capitalized either.

EXERCISE 5: Capitalize the following where necessary.

1. madison high school
2. ford van
3. junior year
4. school holiday
5. a college in trenton
6. spanish
7. the new york daily news
8. columbia university
9. oneida silver company
10. chemistry
11. rice krispies
12. constitution of the united states
13. flynn's television repair service
14. fabric mending tape

RULES FOR TIMES AND EVENTS

Days, Months, and Holidays

RULE 1: Capitalize the names of the days of the week and the months of the year.

We have an appointment for Saturday, March 2.

BUT

See me any weekday.

The word "weekday" is not capitalized since it does not refer to a particular day.

Do not capitalize the names of the seasons.

Our store has autumn, spring, summer, and winter sales.
We take our vacation in the fall.

RULE 2: Capitalize the names of holidays and religious holidays.

>Did you see the fireworks on the Fourth of July?
>Our school closes on Yom Kippur and Good Friday.

BUT

>We close on holy days.

The words "holy days" are not capitalized since they do not refer to particular days.

Special Occasions

RULE 3: Capitalize the names of historical periods and events.

>Many soldiers died during the Revolutionary War.
>We shall study the Renaissance next semester.

RULE 4: Capitalize the names of awards and prizes.

>He won the Nobel Prize in literature.
>How many National Merit Scholars were in the graduating class?

EXERCISE 6: Capitalize where necessary.

1. tuesday
2. christmas eve
3. fall
4. middle ages
5. baseball hall of fame
6. easter
7. all saints' day
8. winter
9. april 9
10. pulitzer prize

EXERCISES FOR REVIEW

A. Capitalize where necessary.

1. benjamin franklin said, "we must all hang together, else we shall all hang separately."
2. among the well-known stories of edgar allan poe are "the murders in the rue morgue" and "the gold bug."

3. another great american writer, emily dickinson, wrote short verses whose titles are their first lines, such as "the pedigree of honey."
4. how many times did abraham lincoln revise his gettysburg address?
5. in some books by louisa may alcott, leading roles are played by her father, mother (whom she called "marmee" in *little women*), and sisters.

B. Capitalize where necessary.

1. sun, stars, and moon
2. london
3. north atlantic
4. the philadelphia inquirer
5. pluto and uranus
6. kansas and nebraska
7. lincoln mercury dealer
8. dinosaur national park
9. union carbide company
10. boston red sox
11. newsweek
12. university of wisconsin at madison
13. french history
14. chinese cuisine
15. u.c.l.a.
16. nato
17. declaration of independence
18. fig newtons

C. Capitalize where necessary.

1. june weather
2. christmas shopping
3. tuesday night
4. winter days
5. june 6, 1944
6. july and august
7. memorial day
8. groundhog day
9. colonial architecture
10. neolithic period
11. franco-prussian war
12. baroque era
13. rhodes scholarship
14. pulitzer prize
15. thanksgiving day
16. fall foliage
17. february 29
18. every sunday

D. Capitalize where necessary.

1. my cousin
2. cousin helen
3. our family doctor
4. christian charity
5. city official
6. new yorkers
7. brother philip
8. jewish friends
9. uncle henry
10. congressman
11. french
12. my mother
13. sun and stars
14. north korea
15. june in january
16. christmas carols
17. down south
18. washington monument

E. Capitalize where necessary.

1. london times
2. doctor henderson
3. nurse
4. democrat
5. portuguese
6. earth
7. ajax fruit company
8. dallas cowboys
9. pacific avenue
10. mathematics
11. autumn
12. easter
13. des moines
14. general science
15. university degree
16. fifth amendment
17. syracuse university
18. monday wash

F. Capitalize where necessary.

      2134 tenth street
      canton, ohio
      april 9, 1985

mr. morris tesso
fourth lake association
hadley, new york 12216

dear mr. tesso:
  in this month's issue of the adirondack guide you suggested we write to you for information about vacation trips.
  our thursday club plans a weekend trip into your area this summer. we are particularly interested in information about camp grounds near indian village and lake george. we would also appreciate receiving a copy of your publication my best fishing days.
  will it be difficult to get accommodations over the fourth of july weekend?

if the weather is usually warm during the early fall, we would consider making a trip at that time.
thanks very much for your help.

        cordially yours,

        margaret haverstraw

G. Capitalize where needed. Add periods at the ends of sentences where necessary.

when the space shuttle challenger blasted off on its eight-day mission, it carried a seven-member crew two women, dr. kathryn sullivan and dr. sally k. ride, were on board dr. sullivan made the first walk in space by an american woman it was dr. ride's second shuttle flight also aboard was comdr. marc garneau of the canadian navy, the first canadian to ride into space shuttle commander capt. robert l. crippen of the navy said that the spacecraft was quite crowded on its inaugural flight a month earlier the space shuttle discovery carried a crew of six a russian space station was home to as many as six astronauts at one time instead of being launched across the atlantic, the challenger was launched in a northeast direction parallel to the coast the launching was visible to those with binoculars as far north as south carolina

11. ABBREVIATIONS

In this chapter you will learn:
1. how to spell abbreviations
2. when to use abbreviations
3. how to identify some commonly used acronyms

ABBREVIATIONS OF NAMES AND TITLES

Titles of Respect

The following titles of respect are always abbreviated:

        Mr.   Mrs.   Ms.   Dr.   St.

The words *doctor* and *saint* are not abbreviated when they are not followed by names:

> The man who wanted to be a doctor ended up writing a book about the death of the saint.

The following may or may not be abbreviated:

    Prof. (Professor)   Rev. (Reverend)
    Hon. (Honorable)   Msgr. (Monsignor)

NOTE: *Miss* is not an abbreviation and therefore is not followed by a period.

The term *Messrs.* (Messieurs) is used when listing more than one *Mr.*

    Messrs. Ryan, Hammond, and Jenks

The term *Mmes.* (Mesdames) is used when listing more than one *Mrs.*

    Mmes. Garvey, Standon, and Furst

Do not abbreviate first names.

>George and William are my cousins. (not Geo. and Wm.)

Titles and Degrees after Names

The abbreviations *Jr., Sr., II, III* (or *2d, 3d*) after a name are part of that name. *Jr.* and *Sr.* are preceded by commas. The other forms are not.

>Mr. George Jefferson, Jr.
>Mrs. Harry Samuels III

The abbreviation *Esq.* (Esquire) is written after a lawyer's name. When using *Esq.* do not use a title before the name.

>Marion Longstreet, Esq.
>Raymond Carter, Esq.

Frequently used abbreviations of scholarly degrees or official positions are:

A.B. or B.A. (Bachelor of Arts)
B.S. (Bachelor of Science)
D.D. (Doctor of Divinity)
D.D.S. (Doctor of Dental Surgery)
J.P. (Justice of the Peace)
C.P.A. (Certified Public Accountant)
LL.D. (Doctor of Laws)
M.A. (Master of Arts)
M.D. (Doctor of Medicine)
Ph.D. (Doctor of Philosophy)
M.P. (Military Police *or* Member of Parliament)
R.N. (Registered Nurse)

These abbreviations follow the name. When they are used, do not use Mr., Mrs., Ms., Miss, or Dr.

>Jackson Printer, D.D.S.
>Marilyn Hess, Ph.D.

Company Names

The following abbreviations are frequently used as parts of firm names:

Bro., Bros. (Brothers)
Co. (Company)
Corp. (Corporation)
Inc. (Incorporated)
Ltd. (Limited)
P.C. (Private Corporation)
& (and)

These abbreviations usually appear at the end of the firm's name.

>Smith & Bros., Inc.
>Winsor Corp.

EXERCISE 1: Write abbreviations for the following in the space provided.

1. Mister Gary Hamilton the third
2. Strong Brothers
3. Jones and Company, Incorporated
4. Stanley Corman, Registered Nurse
5. Mrs. Berenson and Mrs. Goldstein
6. Jonathan Southy, Doctor of Divinity
7. MaryAnn Jimenez, Esquire
8. Monsignor Samuel O'Neill
9. Nancy Astor, Member of Parliament
10. Master of Arts
11. Doctor Johnson
12. Tanner and Swire, Limited
13. Misters Blackburn and Kline
14. Saint Sebastian
15. Alice Carter, doctor of philosophy

PLACES AND TIMES

Geographical Terms

Always spell out names of territories and possessions of the United States if they are standing alone.

> Mike met me in California before going to Hawaii.

State names should also be spelled out when following the name of a city or other geographical term.

> Together we went to Santa Fe, New Mexico.

However, where brevity is desired, as in lists, notes, and indexes, abbreviations may be used. Names of states may be either spelled out or abbreviated in addresses.

There are two standard forms of state abbreviations. The capitalized two-letter form is required by the U.S. postal service and should be used with zip code addresses; the traditional abbreviation is preferred for most other uses where a shortened form is required.

AL Ala. (Alabama)	AK Alaska	AS Amer. Samoa
AZ Ariz.	AR Ark.	CA Calif.
CZ C.Z. (Canal Zone)	CO Colo.	CT Conn.
DE Del.	DC D.C.	FL Fla.
GA Ga.	GU Guam	HI Hawaii
ID Idaho	IL Ill.	IN Ind.
IA Iowa	KS Kans.	KY Ky.
LA La.	MA Mass.	MD Md.
ME Maine	MI Mich.	MN Minn.
MS Miss. (Mississippi)	MO Mo. (Missouri)	MT Mont.
NE Nebr.	NV Nev.	NH N.H.
NJ N.J.	NM N. Mex.	NY N.Y.
NC N.C.	ND N.Dak.	OH Ohio
OK Okla.	OR Oreg.	PA Pa.
PR P.R.	RI R.I.	SC S.C.
SD S.Dak.	TN Tenn.	TX Tex.
UT Utah	VT Vt.	VA Va.
VI V.I.	WA Wash.	WV W.Va.
WI Wis.	WY Wyo.	

The names of nations are usually spelled out in text, but may be abbreviated in lists, bibliographies, etc. Exceptions: The Soviet Union is often abbreviated as USSR; U.S. is used as an adjective in all but the most formal writing:

> In the USSR, exhibits of U.S. art or manufactures are extremely rare events.

EXERCISE 2: (a) Write the approved Post Office (two-letter) abbreviation of each state whose traditional abbreviation is given below.

Ill.	Amer. Samoa
Kans.	Nebr.
La.	Ala.
W. Va.	Tenn.
Wash.	Ark.

(b) Write the name of the state whose two-letter abbreviation is given below.

AZ	NH
ME	IA

HI	MS
AK	MA
TX	TN
MI	MN
MO	MT
DE	OK

Addresses

Spell out addresses when they are in letters or text. You may abbreviate them on an envelope.

Avenue—Ave.   Boulevard—Blvd.   Building—Bldg.
Court—Ct.   Drive—Dr.   Lane—La.
Parkway—Pkwy. Place—Pl.   Road—Rd.
Square—Sq.   Street—St.   Terrace—Terr.
North—N.   South—S.   East—E.
West—W.

Days and Months

Always spell out months of the year and days of the week in letters or text. You may abbreviate them in tables, charts, footnotes.

January—Jan.   February—Feb.   March—Mar.
April—Apr.   August—Aug.   September—Sept.
October—Oct.   November—Nov.   December—Dec.

NOTE: May, June, and July are not abbreviated.

Sunday—Sun.   Monday—Mon.   Tuesday—Tues.
Wednesday—Wed.   Thursday—Thurs.   Friday—Fri.
Saturday—Sat.

EXERCISE 3: Write the abbreviation for each of the following.

1. Court
2. December
3. North Pine Place
4. Tuesday

5. August
7. Square
9. Sunday
6. Boulevard
8. January
10. East Thirty-Third Drive

Time, Numbers, and Dates

Times

The following are examples of the abbreviations commonly used to refer to time zones:

>GMT (or G.M.T.)—Greenwich Mean Time
>EDT (or E.D.T.)—Eastern Daylight Time
>MST (or M.S.T.)—Mountain Standard Time
>PST (or P.S.T.)—Pacific Standard Time

The abbreviations A.M. (for *ante meridiem,* before noon) and P.M. (*post meridiem,* after noon) are always capitalized.

Numbers

Spell out numbers that can be expressed in a word or two; use figures for longer ones.

>after ten years
>less than forty dollars
>after 245 years
>more than $35.67

Do not begin a sentence with a figure.

>Ten people came to the party. (*not* 10 people came to the party.)

Dates

For dates, follow these models:

>April 9, 1958 *or* April 1958 (*not* April 9th, 1958)
>April 8th; eighth of April; April 8
>1950–1955 *or* from 1950 to 1955 *or* 1950–55 (*not* from 1950–1955; *not* from 1950–55)

COMMONLY USED ABBREVIATIONS

Customary Measurement Terms

Length

in.	inch(es)
ft.	foot, feet
yd.	yard(s)
rd.	rod(s)
mi.	mile(s)

Area

sq. in.	square inch(es)
sq. ft.	square foot (feet)
sq. yd.	square yard(s)
sq. rd.	square rod(s)
sq. mi.	square mile(s)
a.	acre

Volume

cu. in.	cubic inch(es)
cu. ft.	cubic foot (feet)
cu. yd.	cubic yard

Measures of Weight and Capacity

Weight

gr.	grain(s)
dr.	dram(s)
oz.	ounce(s)
lb.	pound(s)
tn.	ton(s)

Dry Measure

pt.	pint(s)
qt.	quart(s)
pk.	peck(s)
bu.	bushel(s)

Liquid Measure

fl. oz.	fluid ounce(s)
pt.	pint(s)
qt.	quart(s)
gal.	gllon(s)
bbl.	barrel(s)

Metric Measurement

The metric system of measurement employs three basic units:

m.	meter	unit for length
g.	gram	unit for weight
l.	liter	unit for capacity

These units are combined with the following prefixes, which have the value indicated:

m	milli-	(.001)	dk	deca- or deka-	(10)
c	centi-	(.01)	h	hecto-	(100)
d	deci-	(.1)	k	kilo-	(1,000)

10 decigrams = 1 gram   10 dg. = 1 g.
100 centimeters = 1 meter   100 cm. = 1 m.
10 dekaliters = 1 hectoliter   10 dkl. = 1 hl.

Abbreviations Used in Dictionary Entries

abbr.	abbreviated	abr.	abridged
	abbreviation		abridgement
adj.	adjective	adv.	adverb
ant.	antonym	arch.	archaic
conj.	conjunction	colloq.	colloquial
def.	definition	dict.	dictionary
interj.	interjection	lit.	literally
n.	noun	obs.	obsolete
pl.	plural	prep.	preposition
pron.	pronoun	sing.	singular
syn.	synonym	vi.	intransitive verb
vt.	transitive verb		

EXERCISE 4: Write the abbreviation for each of the following terms.

1. square inch
2. ounces and pounds
3. milliliters
4. kilogram
5. adjective
6. transitive verb
7. cubic feet
8. miles
9. grains
10. bushel and peck
11. literally
12. singular
13. colloquial
14. plural
15. obsolete
16. square yard
17. intransitive verb
18. conjunction

Abbreviations for Charts and Business

The following abbreviations are used in business tabulations, charts, and footnotes. In letters or text, these words should be spelled out.

acct.	account	agt.	agent
bal.	balance	cc.	copy, copies
c/o	care of	copr. or ©	copyright
C.O.D.	cash on delivery	cr.	credit
dept.	department	ea.	each
hq. or hdqrs.	headquarters	mdse.	merchandise
mgr.	manager	mfg.	manufacturing
mfr.	manufacturer	memo	memorandum
M.O.	money order	mtg.	mortgage
mo.	month	pd.	paid
Pres.	President	no.	number
V.P.	Vice President	vs.	against
rec'd	received	yr.	year
wk.	week		

In business correspondence, the following abbreviations are *never* spelled out:

        etc.—et cetera, and so on   P.S.—postscript

EXERCISE 5: The following notes were found on an office memorandum pad. Translate each statement.

1. give 2 cc to dept mgr
2. tell V.P. about M.O. from agt
3. check mdse rec'd last mo
4. is acct bal pd?
5. call hq about no. C.O.D.s
6. how much cr. can I get for mtg?

Publishing and Scholarly Abbreviations

The following abbreviations refer to parts of a manuscript or book:

app.	appendix	art.	article
bk.	book	ch., chap.	chapter
col.	column	ed.	edition
fig.	figure	ex.	example
l.	line	fol.	folio
ll.	lines	n.	note, footnote
p.	page	nn.	notes, footnotes
pp.	pages	par.	paragraph

pl.	plate	pt.	part
sec.	section	ser.	series
st.	stanza	supp.	supplement
v.	verse	vol.	volume

The following Latin abbreviations are used in scholarly works:

ad inf.	*ad infinitum*	to infinity
ad lib.	*ad libitum*	at will
ad loc.	*ad locum*	at the place
bibl.	*bibliotheca*	library (*hence* bibliography)
c., ca.	*circa*	about, approximately
cf.	*confer*	compare
con.	*contra*	against
e.g.	*exempli gratia*	for example
et al.	*et alii*	and others
et. seq.	*et sequentes*	and the following
ibid.	*ibidem*	in the same place
id.	*idem*	the same
i.e.	*id est*	that is
inf.	*infra*	below
loc. cit.	*loco citato*	in the place cited
ms (pl. mss)	*manuscriptum-a*	manuscript(s)
N.B.	*nota bene*	take careful note
non seq.	*non sequitur*	it does not follow
n.	*natus*	born
ob.	*obiit*	died
op. cit.	*opere citato*	in the work cited
pass.	*passim*	throughout
P.S.	*post scriptum*	a postscript
PPS.	*post postscriptum*	a later postscript
pro tem.	*pro tempore*	for the time being
Q.E.D.	*quod erat demonstrandum*	that which has been demonstrated
q.v.	*quod vide*	which see
sic*	*sic*	thus (appeared exactly this way)
sup.	*supra*	above
v.	*vide*	see
viz.	*videlicet*	namely

*Sic is a complete Latin word, usually translated as "thus," and *not* an abbreviation. We include it here because you are likely to see it used along with the true abbreviations on this list.

Some Other Familiar Abbreviations

A.D.	Anno Domini (in the year of [our] Lord)	B. C.	before Christ
C.	Celsius	cal.	calorie
c.	cup	doz.	dozen
cont.	continued	encyc.	encyclopedia
ex.	example	F.	Fahrenheit
kcal.	kilocalorie	mph	miles per hour
M.	mile, thousand	tbs., tbsp.	tablespoon
mt.	mountain	R.S.V.P.	reply requested (from French)
rpm.	revolutions per minute	tsp.	teaspoon

There are many more abbreviations in everyday or specialized use than those we have been able to list in this chapter. When you come across an unfamiliar one, consult your dictionary.

EXERCISE 6: Write the meaning of each of the following abbreviations.

1. vol.
2. 10 A.M.
3. cf.
4. pp.
5. Q.E.D.
6. i.e.
7. op. cit.
8. mt.
9. ed.
10. tbsp.
11. e.g.
12. N.B.
13. r.p.m.
14. fig.
15. ch.
16. ca.
17. et al.
18. ibid.

EXERCISE 7: Write the abbreviation for each of the following terms.

1. Hawaii
2. Certified Public Accountant
3. morning
4. incorporated
5. Doctor of Laws
6. chapter
7. dentist
8. conjunction

9. Bachelor of Arts
10. intransitive verb
11. road
12. teaspoon
13. gallon
14. Friday
15. pages
16. milligram
17. Alabama
18. namely

ACRONYMS

An acronym is a word that is formed from the first or first few letters of a series of words. For example, the word *radar* comes from *ra*dio *d*etecting *a*nd *r*anging.

Organization Names and Other Well-Known Acronyms

There are as many acronyms as there are organizations and government agencies. Some well-known ones are listed below:

AFL-CIO	American Federation of Labor–Congress of Industrial Organizations
AWOL	Absent Without Leave
CARE	Cooperative for American Relief Everywhere
DOA	Department of Agriculture; Dead on Arrival
DOD	Department of Defense
DHHS	Department of Health and Human Services
FCC	Federal Communications Commission
FDA	Food and Drug Administration
FTC	Federal Trade Commission
NASA	National Aeronautics and Space Administration
NATO	North Atlantic Treaty Organization
NET	National Educational Television
NLRB	National Labor Relations Board
PAL	Police Athletic League
PBS	Public Broadcasting System
SALT	Strategic Arms Limitations Talk
SEATO	Southeast Asia Treaty Organization
smog	Smoke and Fog
UN or U.N.	United Nations
UNICEF	United Nations International Children's Emergency Fund
UNESCO	United Nations Economic, Social and Cultural Organization

154 / Mastering Spelling

VISTA   Volunteers in Service to America
WHO   World Health Organization

Some Commonly Used Computer Acronyms

APL   A Programming Language
ASCII   American Standard Code for Information Interchange
ATM   Automatic Teller Machine
BASIC   Beginner's All-Purpose Symbolic Instruction Code (a programming language)
bit   contraction of "binary digit"
BPI   Bytes per inch (a byte is a group of eight bits)
CRT   Cathode Ray Tube (monitor or screen)
CPU   central processing unit
COBOL   Common Business-Oriented Language
COM   Computer Output Microfilm
DBMS   Data Base Management System
DP   Data Processing
EDP   Electronic Data Processing
FORTRAN   Formula Translation (a programming language)
GIGO   Garbage In–Garbage Out
I/O   Input/Output Device
K, KB   Kilobytes or thousand bytes
MICR   Magnetic Ink Character Recogniton
MIS   Managment Information System
OCR   Optical Character Recognition
OS   Operating System
PC   Personal Computer
PL/I   Programming Language I
RAM   Random-Access Memory
ROM   Read-Only Memory
TPI   Tracks Per Inch
UPS   Uninterrupted Power Supply
WP   Word Processing (or Processor)

EXERCISE 8: Rewrite the following advertisements and headlines, spelling out all the underlined acronyms.

1. HELP WANTED: EDP programmer. Must know COBOL, FORTRAN.
2. New PC! 128 K RAM. 9-in. CRT. Comes with DOS, BASIC, more.
3. AFL-CIO CHIEF TO MEET FCC AND FTC

4. SMOG ROLLS IN FROM NATO, SEATO, SAYS PBS REPORT
5. MIS executives! Compare our DBMS. Comes with windows, integrated filing, WP, graphics. Recommended by DOA, NLRB.

EXERCISES FOR REVIEW

A. Write the word or expression for which each abbreviation is used.

1. Rev.
2. St.
3. Mmes.
4. M.D.
5. Ph. D.
6. Co.
7. P.M.
8. Inc.
9. MI
10. MN
11. Hon.
12. Pkwy.
13. Wed.
14. Nov.
15. Bldg.
16. PDT
17. R.N.
18. Oreg.

B. Write an abbreviation for each of the following terms.

1. Master of Arts
2. more than one mister
3. Hahn Brothers, Limited
4. Louisiana
5. 6 o'clock in the evening
6. Mountain Standard Time
7. Idaho
8. Soto and Sons, Incorporated
9. Justice of the Peace
10. Washington (state)
11. September
12. Saturday
13. 12 North Terrace Drive
14. Bachelor of Science

C. Write an abbreviation for each of the following terms.

1. quart
2. foot
3. liter
4. yard

5. centimeter
6. milliliter
7. gram
8. bushel
9. miles
10. cubic feet
11. kilometers
12. decagram
13. acre
14. square inches
15. pounds
16. pint
17. fl. ounces
18. grains

D. Write the word or expression for which each of the following abbreviations is used.

1. lit.
2. cc.
3. memo
4. yr.
5. app.
6. ad lib.
7. ob.
8. non seq.
9. m.p.h.
10. tsp.
11. id.
12. et seq.
13. cont.
14. mss.
15. pt.
16. supp.
17. mdse.
18. Pres.

E. Write an abbreviation for each of the following.

1. money order
2. care of
3. corporation
4. miscellaneous
5. headquarters
6. quart
7. and
8. month
9. miles per hour
10. paid
11. page
12. example
13. January
14. medical doctor
15. week
16. versus

17.	preposition	18.	New Jersey
19.	each	20.	year

F. Write an abbreviation for each of the following.

1.	adjective	2.	Montana
3.	singular	4.	feet
5.	abbreviation	6.	definition
7.	manager	8.	et cetera (and so forth)
9.	saint	10.	September
11.	Wednesday	12.	noun
13.	cash on delivery	14.	reply requested
15.	adverb	16.	pronoun
17.	hour	18.	Vice President
19.	tablespoon	20.	gallon

G. Write the word or expression for which each of the following abbreviations stands.

1.	A.M.	2.	tsp.
3.	pl.	4.	etc.
5.	i.e.	6.	M.O.
7.	pron.	8.	vt.
9.	vol.	10.	qt.
11.	dkg.	12.	interj.
13.	sing.	14.	sq. yd.
15.	cu. ft.	16.	cc.
17.	cm.	18.	abbr.

H. What do the following acronyms represent?

1.	UN	2.	CARE
3.	USSR	4.	UNICEF

5. NATO
7. NASA
9. PAL

6. AFL-CIO
8. SALT
10. AWOL

I. Define the following computer terms.

1. BPI
3. ATM
5. GIGO
7. OS
9. KB

2. APL
4. EDP
6. MIS
8. RAM
10. PC

J. The sales manager took the following notes at a meeting. Write them out in full.

Mon., Sept. 5
Memo to staff: Things to do:
    1. dept. heads
    send report ea. mo. to hq. with mdse. sales figs.
    2. V.P.
    get cc. of cr. memo. send to mfr c/o acct. no. 7
    3. office mgr.
    get copy of C.O.D. invoice from mfg. dept.
    add following names to mailing list:
    Rev. Wm. Hammond
    Jack Lawson, J.P.
    Loretta Stevens, Ph.D.
    Prof. Jeanne Montgomery
    4. handyman
    build storage cabinet 5 ft. by 3 ft.
    check inventory of pt. and qt. containers
    5. typist
    check app. in bk. for changes
    renumber ea. chap.
    count ll. in par. 3, p. 14
    submit bill for last wk. to agt.
    6. D P mgr.
    Can we get © on new DBMS?

12. SPELLING LISTS

A youngster was once asked by his teacher to spell the word "weather." He stood up slowly, took a deep breath, and said, "W-A-H-I-T-U-R."

The teacher couldn't believe what she had heard. "Tommy," she said, "that is the worst spell of weather we've had around here for years."

As you know, spelling many English words can be difficult. After studying the chapters in this book, though, you should be familiar with silent letters, combinations of letters that are pronounced differently in different words, and many of the other patterns that lead to spelling pitfalls. By now you should feel confident that you can spell correctly many words that used to cause you trouble.

This chapter will give you the opportunity to review some of the "trouble-makers" that we have examined in earlier chapters. It also will give you practice in correctly spelling numerous words that have been found to be spelling problems for many people. First, though, we will point out some differences between American English and British English spellings, and look at lists of words that relate to specific subject areas.

In this chapter you will:

1. learn some differences between British and American spellings.
2. study lists of words relating to science and technology, politics and government, the arts, and the business world
3. review the spelling of more than three hundred words that many people find troublesome

There are several ways to make use of the word lists in this chapter. You can have someone dictate the words to you and mark those you spell incorrectly. Then you would have to study only the ones you guessed (!) wrong or missed. The exercises that follow would serve as a review. You also can study the lists alone and then test yourself from the exercise. Or you might want to begin with the exercises and list the words you spelled incorrectly or are unsure of for further study.

Either way, you will end up with a list of words you need to work on. That list will become your own personal Spelling List. Cross words off the list as you master them. But be sure to add new words that you find troublesome.

Good luck!

BRITISH AND AMERICAN SPELLING

Do you go to the theatre (or theater), enjoy its humour (or humor), and become paralysed (or paralyzed) by an audience's poor behaviour (or behavior) especially while sitting in a draught (or draft)?

As you may have guessed by now, our English-speaking relatives in Great Britain prefer *re* to *er*, *our* to *or*, *se* or *ze*, and *au* to *a*. They also buy jewellery (rather than jewelry), even though they, like us, may have to bounce a cheque (not check) to do it.

Because you may find British spelling in your reading—you most certainly will find them in British books and magazines—you should review the lists below for some of the more frequently used words.

A. American *er*—British *re*

- center/centre
- centimeter/centimetre
- luster/lustre
- meager/meagre
- reconnoiter/reconnoitre
- somber/sombre
- theater/theatre
- caliber/calibre
- fiber/fibre
- maneuver/maneuvre
- meter/metre
- sepulcher/sepulchre
- specter/spectre

B. American *ize, yze*—British *ise, yse*

- analyze/analyse
- apologize/apologise
- dramatize/dramatise
- paralyze/paralyse
- sympathize/sympathise

C. American *or*—British *our*

- behavior/behaviour
- clamor/clamour
- endeavor/endeavour
- flavor/flavour
- honor/honour
- labor/labour
- rumor/rumour
- vigor/vigour
- candor/candour
- color/colour
- favor/favour
- harbor/harbour
- humor/humour
- neighbor/neighbour
- splendor/splendour

D. Additional American and British Differences

- ax/axe
- cozy/cosy
- program/programme
- jeweler/jeweller
- mustache/moustache
- check (money)/cheque
- draft/draught
- gray/grey
- jewelry/jewellery
- syrup/sirup

skeptic/sceptic   skeptical/sceptical
smolder/smoulder   canceled/cancelled
focused/focussed

EXERCISE 1: Which of the following are preferred American and which are preferred British spellings? Write *Am* or *Br* as appropriate.

1. meter
2. odour
3. neighbour
4. calibre
5. apologize
6. meager
7. dramatize
8. humor
9. theatre
10. cheque
11. grey
12. skeptic
13. cosy
14. focused
15. programme

FOUR SPECIAL SPELLING LISTS

Each of the four lists that follow contains words related to a specific subject area. If you are interested in music and the theater, you are likely to come across many of the words in the Arts list in your reading. If you are planning to study biology or computer science, you undoubtedly will have to read many of the words on the Science and Technology list. Planning a career in the business world? Don't miss the list that can help you spell *customers* and *management*, *personnel* and *financier*. Whether you are going to lead a consumers' activist group, run for office, or simply be an informed citizen, you'll find *convention* and *caucus*, *proposal* and *privilege* in the list of words relating to Politics and Government. Ready, set, go!

The Arts

choreographer
traditional
rehearsal
soprano
autobiographical

musician
musicologist
proofreader
cinematic
grotesque

eclectic
improvisation
pirouette
memoir
connotation

idiosyncracy
fantasies
apparel
curator
monumental

museum
inspiration
literature
heterogenous
denouement

philosophical
costume
exhibition
elaboration
collaboration

acclaim   playwright   designer
publicity   danceable   artificial
epic   achievement   professional
irrational   creativity   ambiguous
ideology   translation   illusory

virtuoso   performance   script
cue   contributor   cello
bass   harpsichord   eloquence
alto   tenor   Renaissance
conductor   percussion   instrument

Science and Technology

genetics   clone   energize
cassette   high-fidelity   stereophonic
videodisc   cable   programming
electronics   meteorology   mineralogy
research   environment   nutrition

technology   engineer   development
conservation   consumer   invention
pollution   psychology   science
additives   software   functional
digital   simulator   compatibility

manual   automatically   mechanism
ignition   artificial   transmission
component   sensitivity   dimensions
defective   monitoring   microphone
circuitry   encoded   audiophile

documentation   ecology   anthropology
demographics   electricity   nuclear
biotechnology   archeology   statistical
component   printout   breakthrough
satellite   niche   quantum

Business

accommodate   accounts   advertising
affairs   annually   budget
business   certificate   committee
communication   payroll   conglomerate
cooperation   cordially   correspondence

customers	decision	delivery
department	discussions	employment
estimate	executive	financial
freight	instructions	insurance
judgment	management	memorandum
merchandise	mortgage	organization
personnel	purchased	quantity
records	recruit	reference
renewal	replying	response
revenue	schedule	secretary
shipping	sincerely	statement
superintendent	supervisor	receivables
verify	withdrawal	employees
acquisition	financier	manufacturer
analysis	inflationary	invoices

Politics and Government

caucus	administration	electorate
convention	compromise	association
argument	ascertain	authority
benefit	boundary	bulletin
bureau	campaign	censorship
citizens	commission	community
constituent	justice	military
minority	majority	official
president	cabinet	representatives
recession	paradox	propaganda
registration	delegates	campaign
issues	politician	charisma
license	diplomatic	election
grievances	government	resignation
ambitious	bureaucrats	diversity
constitution	by-laws	negotiation
tariff	poll	unanimously
proposal	deficit	Congress
parliament	privilege	Capitol
legislature	assembly	diplomacy

THE MOST DIFFICULT WORDS TO SPELL

Here they are—the words that people seem to find difficult to spell correctly! However, not everyone has trouble with all of these words. Many will be a breeze for you. If possible, get someone to dictate the words to you, one group at a time. See which ones you have trouble with, and mark them on the list. Perhaps several students can get together and take turns reading groups of words to each other.

Double Trouble

Here is a list of the most frequently misspelled words that contain double letters:

misspell	immediate	suggestion
embarrass	accommodate	committee
exaggerate	recommend	occasion
ammunition	opposite	grammar
bookkeeper	personnel	unnecessary
hurriedly	guarantee	session
interrupt	occurred	success
vacuum	warrant	

The Problem Words

agreeable	loose	beginning
actually	laid	answer
resistance	instead	ache
substantial	hoarse	generation
liberation	half	besiege
guess	forty	diploma
though	February	description
sugar	enough	celery
straight	country	capacity
separate	cough	brief
immense	league	equipped
hygiene	knowledge	enormous
height	independent	divide
guilty	magazine	occasion
gratitude	lightning	ninth

Spelling Lists

beautiful
approval
arrange
clothes
sufficient

articles
principles
exception
temporary
specified

lovingly
planned
realize
difficulty
university

spirits
advisable
completely
special
determine

good-bye
endeavor
practice
permanent
proposition

consequently
style
gentlemen
entirely
transferred

existence
regretting
situation
accordingly
omitted

later
stating
considerably
opportunities
handling

future
grateful
disposition
acquaintance
connection

acknowledgment
assistant
lately
gamble
fiercely

perfectly
happened
ridiculous
conscience
length

society
loss
almost
partial
especially

military
civilian
compensation
expensive
elite

lose
through
friend
disguise
accurate

particularly
effect
enough
sensuous
tomorrow

edition
inconvenience
satisfactorily
personally
concerning

invitation
develop
volume
national
relief

hospital
sympathy
distribution
altogether
drawn

double
generally
dormitory
minimum
easily

applicant
residency
security
demolition
involvement

privilege
combatant
enzyme
pacifist
education

exhausted
individual
dining
terribly
appearance

recently
merely
interested
approximately
extension

view
various
cancellation
receiving
doubt

circumstances	surprised	duplicate
actually	excellent	balance
suppose	different	definitely
criticism	disappointed	experience
supply	purpose	extremely
promptly	necessity	apparently
affectionately	courtesy	service
appreciation	certainly	information
exceedingly	inquiry	therefore
although	canceled	hoping
all right	accept	undoubtedly
bearing	mentioned	absolutely
assume	obliged	until
addressed	mutual	either
semester	possibility	quite
finally	forwarded	assuring
familiar	ordered	opinion
exhibit	guardian	duly
excellent	surely	library
owing	pleasant	leisure
practically	choose	studying
faculty	built	explanation
unfortunately	believe	effort
stereotype	preceded	preferred
stationery	poignant	intelligible
evidently	naturally	grateful
satisfied	allowed	gradually
relative	prior	formula
originally	stationary	foreign
attached	souvenir	thoroughly
inept	awfully	candor
idealized	convenience	aviation
holocaust	referred	complication
gambol	regarding	arduous
disease	enclosed	nephew
pictorial	bicycle	contemporary
phonetic	banana	radical
paternal	athlete	quiet
option	valuable	preoccupation
launch	usually	occupy

piece	believe	attention
often	pleasure	course
academy	probably	least
truly	deficiency	exactly
trouble	guess	stopped
unusual	earliest	latter
temperature	ought	anxious
similar	necessary	available
ninety	sanitary	impossible
niece	physician	entitled
accident	error	laudable
realize	envelope	lapse
divide	accept	international
thought	welfare	rarified
absence	variety	dilemma
folks	physical	following
character	peculiar	additional
colonies	neither	credited
proceeded	cliché	medicine
various	census	material

13. MASTERY TESTS

This chapter contains three kinds of tests. These tests will help you to determine how well you have learned the spelling skills discussed in the previous chapters of this book. Part I of this chapter contains four Mixed Mastery tests that you can do alone. Part II of this chapter contains eight sets of Word Groups that will also let you test your spelling skills alone. Part III, Dictations, contains a variety of exercises that should be dictated to you. If you have been using this book in a self-study program, you may want to ask a friend to dictate some of these exercises to you. Another possibility is for a group of students to take turns dictating the exercises to one another. In a class, of course, the instructor will probably be the person who dictates these exercises. (See A Note to the Examiner on page 179 for more information about using the exercises in Part III.)

I. MIXED MASTERY

A.

1. Write the contractions of the following words. For example, *I will* would be written *I'll*.

you will	are not
would not	I am
I have	you are
have not	it is
that is	I have

2. Write the plural form of each of these words.

woman	copy
tomato	knife
chief	mouse
moose	fish
calf	baby

3. Write the word or expression for which each of the abbreviations stands.

p. o.	mo.
A. M.	oz.
sq. yd.	etc.

4. Arrange these words in alphabetical order.

rebel, razor, realization, recess, raze, reaper, reach, recent, recipe, recount

B.

1. Arrange these words in alphabetical order.

patter, patient, patent, patron, past, pasture, pastry, partly, partridges, parlor

2. Write the abbreviation for each word.

mister	boulevard
morning	received
pound	doctor
afternoon	meter
square foot	manuscript

3. Write the plural form of each of these words.

cliff	banana
puff	ax
radio	eye
lamb	rush
valley	tobacco

4. Change the meaning of each word to its opposite by adding a prefix.

important	probable
regular	agreeable
direct	

C.

1. Write the plural form of each of the following words.

platoon	leaf
lady	fox
mosquito	country
person	wolf
loaf	ox

2. Change the meaning of each word to its opposite by adding a prefix.

perfect	correct
natural	personal
legal	

3. Write the word or expression for which each of the following abbreviations stands.

Hon.	Ph. D.
C.O.D.	Jan.
Mon.	et al.
pp.	R.S.V.P.
tbsp.	ml

4. Arrange these words in alphabetical order.

dainty, date, daily, dairy, damage, dark, danger, Dakota, dawn, daisy

D.

1. Write the plural form of each of the following words.

potato	valley
enemy	pony
cliff	thief
foot	solo
sheep	bush

2. Write out the expressions for which each of the following is a contraction.

couldn't	won't
it's	can't
she'll	we're
haven't	aren't
where's	who's

3. What language is spoken in each of the following countries?

Norway	Sweden
Denmark	Finland
Greece	

4. Arrange these words in alphabetical order.

friendship, foundation, film, fundamental, financial, fountain, freight, flying, freeze, flavor

II. WORD GROUPS

A. In each set of words, find the misspelled word if there is one and write it correctly. If no word is misspelled, write "no error." No set contains more than one misspelled word.

1. muscle
   musicle
   corpuscle
   no error

2. operate
   accurate
   composate
   no error

3. possible
   honorible
   eligible
   no error

4. manual
   total
   official
   no error

5. sincerely
   regularely
   genuinely
   no error

6. hamer
   inform
   mature
   no error

7. verrify
   quarrel
   balloon
   no error

8. bravery
   robbery
   militery
   no error

9. preferred
   offerred
   conferred
   no error

10. relieved
    liesure
    niece
    no error

11. majorities
    qualities
    families
    no error

12. occupent
    obedient
    government
    no error

13. indicate
    definate
    separate
    no error

14. celebration
    invation
    quotation
    no error

15. happiness
    loneliness
    sadness
    no error

16. baker
    auditer
    carpenter
    no error

172 / Mastering Spelling

B. In each set of words below, find the misspelled word if there is one and write it correctly. If no word is misspelled, write "no error." No set contains more than one misspelled word.

1. permanence
   endurence
   reminiscence
   no error

2. terrible
   minnute
   interrupt
   no error

3. estimates
   services
   strengthes
   no error

4. visable
   considerable
   agreeable
   no error

5. sailor
   boxor
   aviator
   no error

6. opposate
   estimate
   fortunate
   no error

7. realy
   scarcely
   jealously
   no error

8. lightening
   broadening
   happening
   no error

9. mineral
   electoral
   candal
   no error

10. minuscule
    minuet
    minimum
    no error

11. attendant
    amendmant
    accountant
    no error

12. February
    library
    libarty
    no error

13. academies
    associates
    affairs
    no error

14. strenuous
    continous
    callous
    no error

15. occasion
    impresion
    vision
    no error

16. lable
    dimple
    sample
    no error

C. In each set of words, find the misspelled word if there is one and write it correctly. If no word is misspelled, write "no error."

1. permission
   profession
   separassion
   no error

2. basement
   investment
   arrogent
   no error

3. frieght
   shriek
   piece
   no error

4. activity
   depravity
   ability
   no error

5. greenery
   brewery
   dictionery
   no error

6. superceed
   succeed
   proceed
   no error

7. disease
   repose
   supose
   no error

8. bootted
   patted
   petted
   no error

9. convenience
   courtesy
   distinguish
   no error

10. employer
    partner
    operater
    no error

11. cooperate
    millitary
    blizzard
    no error

12. tobaco
    business
    country
    no error

13. fickle
    brittle
    arrivle
    no error

14. delivary
    necessary
    auxiliary
    no error

15. sensable
    permissible
    adorable
    no error

16. handkercheif
    height
    deceive
    no error

D. In each set of words, find the misspelled word if there is one and write it correctly. If no word is misspelled, write "no error." No set contains more than one misspelled word.

1. arguement
   agreement
   sediment
   no error

2. believe
   achieve
   reciept
   no error

3. liable
   contemptable
   pleasurable
   no error

4. secretary
   millinary
   granary
   no error

5. separate
   definate
   indicate
   no error

6. declaration
   meducation
   compation
   no error

7. tomatto
   tennis
   boycott
   no error

8. terrible
   interrupt
   summarry
   no error

9. ilegal
   renovate
   telegraph
   no error

10. elegance
    abundance
    insistance
    no error

11. hesitate
    duplicate
    investigate
    no error

12. organizor
    counselor
    supervisor
    no error

13. icical
    journal
    corporal
    no error

14. finally
    actually
    definitelly
    no error

15. synonym
    antonym
    colum
    no error

16. tight
    fright
    sight
    no error

E. In each set of words, find the misspelled word if there is one and write it correctly. If no word is misspelled, write "no error." No set contains more than one misspelled word.

1. luminescance
   remembrance
   entrance
   no error

2. mentor
   paintor
   actor
   no error

3. lable
   sample
   dimple
   no error

4. position
   disapoint
   despoil
   no error

5. desirible
   indivisible
   legible
   no error

6. confetion
   question
   composition
   no error

7. arrogantly
   safly
   formerly
   no error

8. grocery
   celery
   boundery
   no error

9. couragous
   infamous
   ambitious
   no error

10. foreign
    rein
    preist
    no error

11. repression
    condission
    concession
    no error

12. efficient
    grammar
    bannana
    no error

13. blosom
    society
    balance
    no error

14. timeless
    timely
    timliness
    no error

15. agitator
    debator
    monitor
    no error

16. gratitude
    amplitude
    exude
    no error

Mastering Spelling

F. In each set of words, find the misspelled word if there is one and write it correctly. If no word is misspelled, write "no error." No set contains more than one misspelled word.

1. tough
   roof
   through
   no error

2. imitation
   initiation
   invitation
   no error

3. efficient
   recalcitrent
   convenient
   no error

4. laboratory
   contradictory
   surgory
   no error

5. carrier
   bearer
   objecter
   no error

6. receive
   mischief
   variety
   no error

7. breakage
   orange
   cabage
   no error

8. recommend
   difficult
   proffit
   no error

9. gnat
   gnot
   gnome
   no error

10. noticable
    applicable
    durable
    no error

11. bouquet
    unquiet
    requiem
    no error

12. annually
    equally
    evidentally
    no error

13. kneel
    knead
    knear
    no error

14. questionible
    permissible
    terrible
    no error

15. exactly
    attentivly
    absolutely
    no error

16. handel
    lapel
    rebel
    no error

G. In each set of words, find the misspelled word if there is one and write it correctly. If no word is misspelled, write "no error." No set contains more than one misspelled word.

1. reign
   neither
   freind
   no error

2. description
   discretion
   impretion
   no error

3. audable
   serviceable
   comparable
   no error

4. begrudge
   tarif
   celery
   no error

5. knight
   knell
   gnash
   no error

6. adjutent
   agent
   superintendent
   no error

7. elementory
   satisfactory
   territory
   no error

8. inventer
   player
   computer
   no error

9. misstake
   baggage
   ellipse
   no error

10. Wednesday
    depot
    solemn
    no error

11. further
    farther
    father
    no error

12. efficiently
    popularly
    accidentally
    no error

13. respectfully
    referral
    relivving
    no error

14. dirigible
    comfortible
    incorrigible
    no error

15. financial
    official
    politicial
    no error

16. evaluate
    educate
    favorate
    no error

H. In each set of words, find the misspelled word if there is one and write it correctly. If no word is misspelled, write "no error." No set contains more than one misspelled word.

1. lier
   sayer
   flier
   no error

2. half
   salmon
   column
   no error

3. squirel
   document
   enclose
   no error

4. composite
   opposite
   estimite
   no error

5. manageable
   peaceable
   loveable
   no error

6. ostrich
   stich
   sandwich
   no error

7. interpretition
   ammunition
   perdition
   no error

8. officer
   oppresser
   commuter
   no error

9. bone
   lamb
   comb
   no error

10. acommodate
    grammar
    recommend
    no error

11. dept
    depth
    width
    no error

12. whistle
    wrinkle
    cancle
    no error

13. beleive
    beseige
    befriend
    no error

14. hymn
    limb
    climb
    no error

15. antler
    gender
    surender
    no error

16. psalm
    briscle
    listen
    no error

III. DICTATIONS

A Note to the Examiner: The remainder of the exercises in this chapter are to be dictated. Point values have been assigned only for your convenience in combining exercises to suit your testing needs. Exercise sets A and B contain a mixture of item types. Exercises C through H consist of passages to be read aloud to students. Exercises I through L contain lists of words for traditional spelling tests. Note that all words contained in the spelling list on pages 164 through 167 are included in the exercises in Part III.

A.

1. The following words are to be dictated and used in sentences to make the meaning clear. The student should write out each word and then write its abbreviation.   [10]

December
avenue
department
railroad
pound

2. The examiner should dictate the following without emphasizing or otherwise indicating the italicized words. The student should write the entire paragraph. Only the italicized words should be considered in rating the score.   [10]

"*Weigh* the anchor and unfurl the *sail!*" shouted the skipper. With a *fair* breeze and a *straight course* he *knew* he could overtake *their* boat before it *passed through* the channel out to *sea*.

3. Each of the following words is to be dictated. The student is to use each word in a sentence.   [15]

birth, beyond, batter, beef, bead

4. The following words are to be dictated and used in sentences by the examiner to make the meaning clear.   [25]

assuring	contemporary	credited
opinion	radical	medicine
duly	quiet	material
international	studying	attention
rarified	explanation	course
dilemma	effort	least
exactly	preoccupation	library
stopped	occupy	leisure

B.

1. The following word pairs are to be shown to the student. The student must choose one word in each pair and write a sentence. (Credit 2 points for each correct sentence.)   [10]

bury/berry	seam/seem
tide/tied	waste/waist
fair/fare	

2. The examiner should dictate the following without emphasizing or otherwise indicating the italicized words. The student should write the entire paragraph. Only the italicized words should be considered in the score.   [10]

   The inventions of the *past* seventy-five *years* are the results of research over a long *period* of time. *Scientists* have learned a *great* deal about the *composition* of different kinds of matter, about light and *electricity*. *Practical* inventors have made use of the *information which* was collected by the *work* of the scientists.

3. The examiner should dictate the following words and then the student should write the plural form of each word. Only the plural form should be considered in the score.   [10]

family	fish
half	city
corpse	son-in-law
pailful	turkey
inch	shelf

4. The following words are to be dictated and used in sentences by the examiner to make the meaning clear.   [25]

complication	option	piece
arduous	launch	often
nephew	colonies	academy
sensuous	proceeded	excellent
remembrance	various	owing
stating	until	accordingly
considerably	either	omitted
opportunities	quite	later

C.

The examiner should dictate the following without emphasizing or otherwise indicating the italicized words. The student should write the entire paragraph. Only the italicized words should be considered in the score.

1. In almost all *athletic* activities there is some *risk* of *accident* and *injury*. But no one wants us to stop playing *games*. *Better* even a *broken* leg now and then than to be *afraid* to play. It is better still to learn to *protect ourselves* and others. [10]

2. "How shall I go about *planning* my *future?*" "What *career* shall I follow?" These are two perplexing *questions* that all *individuals* must face sooner or later. With few *exceptions,* most of us *naturally* desire to enter and *succeed* in some form of service-producing and wage-earning pursuit. However, young men and women too often fail to get the *necessary information* about their own *abilities* and the many occupational *opportunities* in the world. Thus without chart or compass they obviously are unprepared to make an intelligent *choice,* even of the general type of vocation on which their future *happiness* and success so *largely* depend. [15]

3. All *human* beings have needs that must be *satisfied.* The three most *common* and urgent kinds of needs of all people are food, *clothing,* and *shelter.* The number of such needs *usually increases* as *societies* become more *complex.* For example, the *inhabitants* of *Central* American *tropical forests* are able to get along on wild fruit such as *bananas, some* fish or wild *fowl,* and a few plants. However, people in our society *consume* many kinds of foods, as is *evident* from the *various* items to be found in the weekly menus for an *ordinary* family. [20]

4. In the time of the *colonies* there was very little trading. The roads were few and in poor *condition*. There were no *railways* and no *opportunities* on many of the farms to make use of boats and *water transportation. People* had to be *independent,* that is to say, *sufficient* unto *themselves.* The farm was not *merely* a place for raising livestock, *poultry,* grain, *vegetables,* and fruit; it was also a *factory* in *which* almost *everything* needed in *daily* life was made. A farm family produced the raw *materials* and *also* made them into *useful articles.* Generally speaking, these articles included: wearing apparel and *household fabrics,* various implements, utensils, *furniture,* necessities and comforts, farm tools, *building* materials and other supplies usually needed on the farm. [25]

D.

The examiner should dictate the following without emphasizing or otherwise indicating the italicized words. The student should write the entire paragraph. Only the italicized words should be considered in the score.

1. *Brand* names are important, whether they actually should be or **not.** *Time* magazine once asked an *automobile* industry *marketing executive* what exactly makes a good product name. The *answer* was, "A good name *ought* to *create* a surge of *satisfaction* in the owner when he hears it spoken." Fair *enough.* But how *often* does that happen? I feel exactly nothing when I hear the name of my Mazda spoken.   [10]

2.   I think that if I get into the habit of writing a bit about what *happens,* or rather doesn't happen, I may lose a little of my sense of *loneliness* and *desolation.* A written *monologue* by that most interesting being, *myself,* may have its *consolations.* I shall at *least* have it all my own way. It may bring *relief* as an *outlet* to that *geyser* of emotions, *sensations,* speculations, and *reflections* which *ferments perpetually* within my poor old *carcass.*   [15]

3. *Every change* of *season,* every change of *weather,* indeed, every hour of the day, *produces* some change in the magical hues and shapes of the Catskill *mountains.* They are *regarded* by all, far and near, as perfect barometers. When the weather is *fair* and *settled,* they are *clothed* in *blue* and *purple,* and print *their* bold *outlines* on the *clear evening* sky. Sometimes, when the rest of the landscape is *cloudless,* they will gather a hood of gray vapors about their summits, *which,* in the last rays of the setting sun, will light up like a crown of *glory.*   [20]

4. There's *music* in the air—yes, and shouts and *murmurs,* too, and signals from *airplanes* and a *thousand* other sounds flashing over land and sea in *invisible* waves. We have only to *stretch* out our wire *fingers* and draw the sounds into our very rooms. *Millions* of dollars are spent *annually* in *putting* on the air some of the finest *musical* and *acting talent* in the *country. Concerts* by *orchestras* and noted singers and even whole *operas* are *broadcast. Dramas* with distinguished actors are *presented frequently.* All of this you can *actually enjoy* for nothing if you have access to a *radio* or a *television* set.   [25]

E.

The examiner should dictate the following without emphasizing or otherwise indicating the italicized words. The student should write the entire paragraph. Only the italicized words should be considered in the score.

1. In the *theater actors* become story *characters,* with the help of *lighting* and sound *effects, scenery* and costumes. The story itself becomes a living thing in action and lines of dialogue or *conversation.* Thus we both see and hear the development of the story, while our *imaginations examine* every *detail* of character, action, and plot.   [10]

2. The problem with the fifty-fifty *marriage ideal* lies in the *unrealistic notions* many *people* have of it. No two people can split a marriage in half as if it were an apple. No two people can be *identical* in *emotions, interests,* or *responsibilities*. And no two people can divide their *authorities* and skills in some identically "fair" way. But emotional *equality*—where both *partners* feel *equally* loved, share in family *decisions,* and feel they *contribute* equally to the family's well-being—is the kind of equality that really works.   [15]

3. For a *century* or more the *American people* have believed in *universal education* of *children.* Now we are *coming* to *believe* that education *continues* as long as life. We can not pack all of our learning into a *few* short years. We must keep on learning as long as we live. *Quite* aside from the formal training *courses* conducted by schools and *colleges,* we have the educational *advantages* of *libraries, magazines,* and *daily* papers, and the training conferences and conventions of all the *religious,* educational, civic, *social,* fraternal, and *business* associations. In a sense, we are a nation going to school.   [20]

4. The flag is not just a *piece* of bright *material*. It is the symbol of a great nation. It *deserves* to be *displayed correctly, reverently.*

The flag should *never* trail in the water, never *touch* the ground or anything *beneath* it. It is never *laid* flat. The only *exception* is when it covers the coffin of one who has *served* in our armed *services.*

The flag *should* be half-staffed only for persons who have once *offered* their lives in its *defense*—never for any other person except by Presidential *authority*. For state or city *officials,* half-staff the state or city flag.

All *persons* not in *uniform* salute a *passing* flag by holding the right hand over the *heart*. If out of doors, men should *remove* the hat and hold it in the *right* hand over the heart.   [25]

F.

The examiner should dictate the following without emphasizing or otherwise indicating the italicized words. The student should write the entire paragraph. Only the italicized words should be considered in the score.

1. There is one kind of *power* in the world *which* it took people a long time to learn to use. That is heat. The *comfort* that comes from a fire and the *usefulness* of fire in cooking were *known* in *earliest* times. But the use of heat to lift *weights* and to save human *strength* was possible only after humans had *traveled* a long way on the road of *invention*.   [10]

2. Studies have shown that people, including many happily married couples, can have *radically* different ideas about *vacations*. One might want to travel to *exotic* places or race around *sightseeing,* while the other wants only the *pleasure* of sleeping late or lounging on the beach. One wants constant *stimulation,* while the other seeks peace and quiet and freedom from the need to *interact* with others. One wants family *togetherness;* the other wants only to *pursue* his or her own *interests.* One wants every moment to be *carefully* planned, while the other *relishes* the idea of *uncommitted* time. When two such people try to vacation *together,* the mix can be emotional *dynamite.*   [15]

3. The years *preceding* 1812 were trying ones. The new *republic* had grown *steadily* since the Revolution, *expanding* in territory and solving *tremendous problems* of state. European *nations* had *extended recognition* to this new country, but England *remained hostile, especially* at sea. The leaders in Washington were *patient*—England was a strong *nation,* ruler of the seas, and as yet the United States was hardly her *equal.* But no *adjustment would* they make and *finally* we went to war. The bombardment of Fort McHenry at Baltimore, *which* inspired the writing of "The Star-Spangled Banner," *occurred* in 1814.   [20]

4. The *misconceptions* that *surround Alaska* are as *vast* as the huge land itself. People think of it as a *landscape* of *perpetual* snow, of *polar* bears, Eskimos, and *igloos.* In fact, the 49th state—one-fifth the size of the rest of the country—includes *temperate zones* as well as *frigid* ones, several *distinct* groups of *native* peoples and no igloos at all, not if the word (which means "house" in one of the Eskimo languages) *connotes* a *dwelling* made of snow blocks. The truth is, Alaskan Eskimos *traditionally* built their homes of sod, driftwood, or sticks and skins. Alaska's real *wealth consists* of *unusually abundant* natural *resources* in *addition* to gold; vast areas of *agricultural* lands; billions of feet of timber; a fishing industry; a *fur* trade; *copper;* and coal.   [25]

G.

The examiner should dictate the following without emphasizing or otherwise indicating the italicized words. The student should write the entire paragraph. Only the italicized words should be considered in the score.

1. *Safety* means not taking *unnecessary,* careless or *foolish* risks. It asks that we do not *invite danger* when there is nothing to be *gained* by it. Safety takes no *chances* from *mere* ignorance or lack of *common sense.*   [10]

2. Why is the rule of law so important in dealing with *terrorism?* Because the most *successful tactic* against terrorists is to recruit them, not to shoot them. To do that, the terrorist must be *confident* that he or she will gain from any amnesty that is offered and be *subjected* only to a firm rule of law. The terrorist must also be turned from the *belief* that *violence* will *advance* a cause. This can only be done by a *demonstration* that a better result lies in the *programs* and *policies* of a *government determined* to treat even its *enemies* with *justice*.   [15]

3. *Goat cheese* may be new to Americans, but it has been *cherished* in *Europe* and the Middle East for *centuries*. In fact, goat cheese has *probably* been known since the *beginning* of animal *husbandry*, around 9000 B.C. Goats and cheese are big in the Bible as well as in Greek *mythology*. David was *delivering* cheese when he encountered Goliath. Ulysses *discovered* the Cyclops' cheeses and *devoured* them in short order. Then he watched as the giant "sat down and milked his goats, and then *curdled half* the milk and set it aside in *wicker baskets*." The Cyclops was no *doubt* making feta, perhaps the most *famous* of the goat cheeses, which is still *pickled* in brine or milk as it was *centuries* ago.   [20]

4. The *average* American today can *expect* to live 74.5 years, or 27 years longer than at the *beginning* of the *century*. By the year 2010 *federal health* authorities *predict* the average American will live to age 78. A long-term study in Alameda *County,* California, *disclosed* a striking relationship between the *death* rate and seven common *health practices:* no smoking of cigarettes; *regular exercise;* use of *alcohol* in *moderation* or not at all; seven or *eight* hours of sleep *nightly; maintaining proper weight;* eating *breakfast;* and no eating *between* meals. People who follow only one to three of these practices will die early at two or three times the rate of those who follow them all.   [25]

H.

The examiner should dictate the following without emphasizing or otherwise indicating the italicized words. The student should write the entire paragraph. Only the italicized words should be considered in the score.

1. In the Middle Ages the *ceremony* of homage was a *rite* during which a vassal took a *solemn oath* that he would be the "man" of his future lord. He *knelt* down and placed both of his hands between those of his master. His head was *bare,* as it should have been, and he was without his *weapons*. He *swore* that he would use his hands, when they were *released,* and his weapons, when they were restored to him, only in the *service* of his future lord.   [10]

2. What is the *solution* to the problem of *chemicals* in food? In the final *analysis,* the *individual* must be *responsible* for the *purity* and *safety* of the food he or she buys. Every *consumer* can *choose* between pure foods and those bearing *labels* stating they contain *artificial* colors, artificial flavors, and other artificial *ingredients.* If people seek out and demand pure foods without *additives*—which should be clearly listed upon the label—and *insist* upon their right to such foods, the food *industry* will provide them. [15]

3. To wait quietly for equality to be bestowed on women in *athletics* is to wait for *eternity.* A girl whose *basketball* is flat and whose *uniform* is *patched* may well have equality—but only if the boys are playing basketball under the same *circumstances. Generally,* equality can be looked at in *several* ways. There is *complete* equality if there is *identical money,* an identical number of *teams,* and identical *treatment* in every way for *members* of both sexes. If there are only five teams for girls and ten teams for boys, but there are half as many girls in the *school,* that is a *comparable* situation. *Another* kind of comparable situation exists if a school offers *softball* for girls *instead* of *baseball.* Comparability is not the same as complete equality. [20]

4. As he *approached* the stream, his *heart began* to thump; he summoned up, *however,* all his resolution, gave his horse half a *score* of *kicks* in the ribs, and *attempted* to *dash* quickly *across* the bridge; but *instead* of *starting forward,* the old animal made a sidewise *movement* and ran *against* the fence. His fears *increasing* with the *delay,* he jerked the reins on the other side, and kicked lustily with the *contrary* foot. It was all in *vain;* his steed started, it is true, but it was only to *plunge* to the *opposite* side of the road into a thicket. The schoolmaster now bestowed both *whip* and *heel* upon the ribs of old Gunpowder. The horse dashed forward, but came to a stand just by the *bridge,* with a *suddenness* that *nearly* sent his rider sprawling over his head. [25]

I.

The following words are to be dictated and used in sentences by the examiner to make the meaning clear.

1.
- gentlemen
- entirely
- transferred
- good-bye
- endeaver

- practically
- faculty
- unfortunately
- practice
- permanent

- finally
- familiar
- exhibit
- disguise
- accurate

2.
- existence
- regretting
- situation
- acknowledgment
- assistant

- inconvenience
- satisfactorily
- personally
- hospital
- sympathy

- privilege
- tomarrow
- edition
- terribly
- appearance

Mastery Tests / 187

3. particularly   various   approximately
   effect   cancellation   extension
   enouth   receiving   view
   perfectly   double   society
   happened   generally   loss

4. immense   inept   neither
   hygiene   idealized   cliché
   height   accept   census
   guilty   welfare   stationary
   gratitude   variety   souvenir

5. believe   choose   almost
   pleasure   built   partial
   rpobably   believe   especially
   ninth   deficiency   military
   invitation   copying   civilian

J.
The following words are to be dictated and used in sentences by the examiner to make the meaning clear.

1. proposition   recently   handling
   consequently   merely   circumstances
   style   interested   actually
   clothes   exceedingly   national
   sufficient   although   relief

2. interrupt   develop   description
   vacuum   volume   celery
   suppose   promptly   concerning
   criticism   affectionately surprised
   supply   appreciation   excellent

3. different   assume   obliged
   disappointed   addressed   mutual
   purpose   semester   possibility
   accept   all right   inquiry
   mentioned   bearing   canceled

4. distribution   agreeable   beautiful
   altogether   actually   approval
   drawn   resistance   arrange
   folks   ninety   preceded
   character   niece   poignant

5. articles   divide   usually
   principles   thought   temperature
   exception   absence   similar
   temporary   applicant   accident
   besiege   residency   realize

K.

The following words are to be dictated and used in sentences by the examiner to make the meaning clear.

1. spirits   realize   undoubtedly
   advisable   difficulty   absolutely
   completely   university   latter
   special   following   anxious
   determine   additional   available

2. surely   originally   though
   pleasant   attached   sugar
   apparently   enzyme   straight
   service   pacifist   separate
   information   education   specified

3. earliest   naturally   lovingly
   ought   allowed   planned
   separate   prior   substantial
   sanitary   awfully   liberation
   physician   convenience   guess

4. necessity   doubt   lose
   courtesy   duplicate   through
   certainly   balance   friend
   therefore   preferred   laudable
   hoping   intelligible lapse

5. bicycle   compensation forwarded
   banana   expensive   ordered
   athlete   elite   guardian
   foreign   valuable   physical
   thoroughly   usually   peculiar

L.

The following words are to be dictated and used in sentences by the examiner to make the meaning clear.

1. definitely   exhaused   referred
    experience   individual   regarding
    extremely   dining   enclosed
    occupy   impossible   candor
    guess   entitled   aviation

2. diploma   evidently   ridiculous
    ache   satisfied   conscience
    generation   relative   length
    error   beginning   divide
    envelope   answer   occasion

3. grateful   truly   holocaust
    gradually   trouble   gambol
    formula   security   disease
    privilege   demolition   stereotype
    combatant   involvement   stationary

4. lately   dormitory   equipped
    gamble   minimum   enormous
    fiercely   easily   capacity
    loose   instead   brief
    laid   hoarse   half

5. league   future   forty
    knowledge   grateful   February
    independent   disposition   enough
    magazine   acquaintance   country
    lightning   connection   cough

INDEX

Note: Pages whose numbers are given in *italics* contain exercises that are related to the main discussion.

Abbreviations, 142–58, *169, 170, 179*
  acronyms, 54, 136, 153–55, *157–58*
  in addresses, 145
  of business terms, 150
  capitalization rules, 136–37
  of dates, 147
  of days and months, 146
  in dictionary entries, 149
    for foreign languages, 17
    for parts of speech, 12–13
    of usage labels, 17
  of measurements, 148–49
  of names and titles, 142–44
  of numbers, 147
  of place names, 144–46
  in publishing and scholarly writing, 150–51
  of times, 147
Academic degrees, abbreviation of, 143
Accented syllables, doubling rule, 39
Accent marks, 11–12, *20*
Accept/except, 119
Acronyms
  capitalization rules, 136
  forming plurals of, 54
  used for abbreviation, 153–55
Addresses, abbreviation of, 146
Addition/edition, 119
Adjectives
  adverbs formed from, 77–78, *83*
  changing to nouns, 73, *82*
  formed from geographical names, 79–80, *84*
  formed from nouns and verbs, 76–77, 78, *83*
  nouns used as, 90
  of two or more words, 90
Adverbs, formed from adjectives, 77–78, *83*
Affect/effect, 119
Aisle/isle, 104
Allowed/aloud, 104
All ready/already, 104
Allusion/illusion, 119
Alphabetical order, 5–6, *18, 169, 170*
Altar/alter, 104
Antonyms
  in dictionary entries, 16, *22*
  using prefixes to form, 80–81, *84, 169, 170*
Any-, words beginning with, 90
Apostrophe, 61–71
  with contractions, 61–64, *68–69*

  plurals formed with, 54
  to show possession, 64–68, *69*
Arc/ark, 104
Archaic, usage label, 17
Area measures, abbreviations, 148
Ark/arc, 104
Arts, terms used in the, 161–62
Ascent/assent, 104
Assistance/assistants, 119
Awards, capitalization rules, 138

Band/banned, 104
Bare/bear, 105
Base/bass, 105
Beach/beech, 105
Bear/bare, 105
Beat/beet, 105
Beau/bow, 105
Beech/beach, 105
Beliefs/believes, 49 *fn.*
Berry/bury, 105
Berth/birth, 105
Blew/blue, 105
Boar/bore, 105
Books
  abbreviations used for parts of, 150–51
  capitalization of titles, 130
Born/borne, 105
Bough/bow, 105
Bow/beau, 105
Brake/break, 105
Bread/bred, 105
Breve, 9
Bridal/bridle, 106
British spellings, 160–61
Bury/berry, 105
Business terms
  abbreviation of, 150
  spelling list, 162–63
By/buy, 106

-c, words ending in, adding suffixes to, 26, 42–43, *45*
Canvas/canvass, 106
Capacity measures, abbreviations, 148
Capital/Capitol, 106
Capitalization, 129–41
  of first words, 129–30
  in letter-writing, 130–31, *140–41*
  of names and titles of persons, 132
  of names of groups, 133
  of organizations, 135–36
  of place names, 134–35
  of poetry, 130
  of school subjects and printed matter, 136–37
  of terms for the Deity, 131

Capitalization (*continued*)
   of times and events, 137–38, *139*
   of titles of books and other
      compositions, 130
Carat/carrot, 106
Cede, seed, 106
-ceed/-cede/-sede, prefixes used with,
   88–89, *92–93*
Cellar/seller, 106
Cent/scent/sent, 106
Circumflex, 9
Cite/sight/site, 106
Climb/clime, 106
Coarse/course, 107
Colleges, capitalization of, 136
Colloquial, usage label, 17
Colonel/kernel, 107
Combination words. *See also* Compound
   words
   dictionary order, 5
   forming plurals of, 55–56, *59*
Company names
   abbreviations used in, 143
   capitalization of, 135
Compass directions
   capitalization rules, 134
   hyphen not used with, 90
Complement/compliment, 107
Compound words
   forming plurals of, 55–56, *59*
   possessive forms, 65, *69*
   when to use hyphens with, 89–91, *93*
Computer acronyms, 154, *158*
Consonants
   dictionary pronunciations, 9
   doubling rule, 35–42, *44–45*
Contractions, 61–64, *68–69, 168, 170*
Core/corps, 107
Council/counsel, 107
Course/coarse, 107
Creak/creek, 107

Dates, abbreviation of, 147
Days of the week
   abbreviations, 146
   capitalization of, 137
De-, prefix, 87–88, *92*
Dear/deer, 107
Deceased/diseased, 119
Definitions, in dictionary entries, 15
Deity, capitalization of terms for, 131
Desert/dessert, 107
Dew/do/due, 107
Diacritical marks, 7–9, *19*
Dialect, usage label, 17
Dictionary entries, 5–23
   abbreviations used in, 149
   accent marks, 11–12, *20*
   alphabetical order, 5–6, *18, 169, 170*

definitions, 15
division of words into syllables, 10, *20*
etymologies, 17–18, *23*
guide words, 6, *18–19*
homonyms, 14, *21*
irregular forms, 13–14
part of speech labels, 12–13, *20*
pronunciation guides, 7–10, *19*
synonyms and antonyms, 16, *22*
usage labels, 16–17, *22–23*
Die/dye, 107
Dieresis, 9
Dis-, prefix, 86–87, *92*
Diseased/deceased, 119
Do/due/dew, 107
Doe/dough, 108
Doubled consonants
   spelling rules, 35–42, *44–45*
   spelling list, 164
Dual/duel, 108
Due/do/dew, 107
Dye/die, 107
Dyeing/dying, 33

E, silent. *See* Silent *e*
Edition/addition, 119
Effect/affect, 119
Etymology, 17–18, *23*
Envelop/envelope, 120
Every-, words beginning with, 90
Except/accept, 119

Faint/feint, 108
Fair/fare, 108
Find/fined, 108
Fir/fur, 108
Flea/flee, 108
Flew/flue, 108
Flour/flower, 108
For-/fore-, prefixes, 86, *91–92*
For/fore/four, 108
Formally/formerly, 120
Foreign words
   forming plurals of, 52–54
   usage label, 17
Forth/fourth, 108
Foul/fowl, 108
Four/for/fore, 108
Fur/fir, 108

Gait/gate, 109
Geographical terms. *See* Place names
Gilt/guilt, 109
Gorilla/guerrilla, 109
Government, spelling list of words used
   in, 133
Government departments, capitalization
   rules, 133

Grate/great, 109
Groan/grown, 109
Guerrilla/gorilla, 109
Guessed/guest, 109
Guide words, in dictionaries, 6, *18–19*
Guilt/gilt, 109

Hail/hale, 109
Hair/hare, 109
Hall/haul, 109
Hart/heart, 109
Heal/heel, 109
Hear/here, 110
Heard/herd, 110
Heart/hart, 109
Heel/heal, 109
Here/hear, 110
Higher/hire, 120
Him/hymn, 110
Historical documents, capitalization of, 136
Historical periods and events, capitalization of, 138, *139*
Hoarse/horse, 110
Hole/whole, 110
Holidays, capitalization of, 138
Holy/wholly, 110
Homonyms, 102–28, *179, 180*
 in dictionary entries, 14, *21*
 near-homonyms, 119–23, *126–27*
 that are commonly confused, 102–3, *123–24*
 that are commonly used, 103–19, *124–25*
 using etymologies to distinguish, 18
Horse/hoarse, 110
"Hot Pot" game, 100
Hour/our, 110
Hymn/him, 110
Hyphen, forming compound words with, 89–91, *93*
Hyphenated words, forming plurals of, 55–56

I (pronoun), capitalization of, 132
Idle/idol, 110
-ie, wording ending with, 33
Ie/ei words, spelling rules, 26–28, *43*
Illusion/allusion, 119
In/inn, 110
Incite/insight, 110
Irregular plurals
 formation of, 51–55, *58–59*
 possessive, 64–65
Isle/aisle, 104
It's/its, 63, 102

Judgment/judgement, 33

Kernel/colonel, 107
Knew/new, 110
Knight/night, 110
Know/no, 110

Lain/lane, 110
Languages, capitalization of, 136. *See also* Foreign words; British spellings
Latin abbreviations, 151
Lead/led, 111
Length measures, abbreviations, **148**
Lessen/lesson, 111
Letters of the alphabet, forming plurals of, 54
Letter-writing, capitalization rules, 130–31, *133*
Lie/lye, 111
Load/lode, 111
Loan/lone, 111
Loose/lose, 120
-ly, suffix
 adding to words ending in *y,* 28–29
 forming adverbs with, 77–78, *83*
Lye/lie, 111

Macron, 8–9
Made/maid, 111
Mail/male, 111
Main/mane, 111
Mastery tests, 168–89
 abbreviations, 169, 170, 179
 alphabetical order, 169, 170
 contractions, 168, 170
 dictations, 179–89
 finding misspelled words, 171–78
 homonyms, 179, 180
 plurals, 168, 169, 170, 180
Measurements, abbreviation of, 148–49, *155–56*
Meat/meet, 111
Media/medium, 52 *fn.*
Metal/mettle, 111
Metric measures, abbreviations, **148–49**
Miner/minor, 111
Moral/morale, 120
Months
 abbreviation of, 146
 capitalization of, 137
Morn/mourn, 111

Names of groups, capitalization rules, 133
Names of persons. *See also* Proper nouns
 abbreviation rules, 142–43
 capitalization of, 132
Nations
 abbreviation of, 145
 capitalization of, 134
-ness, suffix, 28–29, *31*

New/knew, 110
Night/knight, 110
No-, words beginning with, 90
No/know, 110
Nouns
  adjectives formed from, 76–77
  changing to another noun form, 75–76
  changing to verbs, 75, *82–83*
  ending in *-er,* 37
  formed from adjectives, 73, *82*
  formed from verbs, 73–75, 78, *82*
  possessive forms, 64–65, *69*
  used as adjectives, 90
Numbers
  abbreviation of, 147
  forming plurals of, 54
  with hyphens, 90
  missing, apostrophe for, 63

Obsolete, usage label, 17
Of/off, 120
One/won, 111
Our/hour, 110

Pail/pale, 112
Pain/pane, 112
Pair/pare/pear, 112
Parts of speech
  changing with suffixes, 76–80, *82–84*
  dictionary labels, 12–13, *20*
Passed/past, 112
Peal/peel, 112
Pear/pair/pare, 112
Personal/personnel, 120
Picture/pitcher, 120
Place names
  abbreviation of, 144–46
  capitalization rules, 134–35
  forming adjectives from, 79–80, *84*
Plain/plane, 112
Plurals, 46–60, *168, 169, 170, 180*
  of compound words, 55–56, *59*
  irregular
    in dictionary entries, 13, *21*
    formation of, 51–55, *58–59*
  possessive, 64–65, *69*
  regular, 47–50, *56–58*
Poetic, usage label, 17
Poetry, capitalization rules, 130
Political parties, capitalization of, 133
Politics and government, spelling list, 163
Pore/pour, 112
Possessive pronouns, 67
Possession, use of apostrophe to show, 64–68, *69*
Pray/prey, 112
Pre-/per-, prefixes, 85–86, *91–92*
Precede/proceed, 88

Prefixes
  antonyms formed with, 80–81, *84, 169, 170*
  that cause spelling problems, 85–89, *91–93*
Present participle, formation of, 78–79, *83*
Principal/principle, 112
Printed matter, capitalization rules, 136
Prizes, capitalization of, 138
Proceed/precede, 88
Profit/prophet, 112
Pronunciation, 94–101
  commonly mispronounced words, 94–95, *99*
  dictionary guides, 7–10, *19–20*
  different spellings that sound alike, 95–97, *99–100*
  letter combinations with different pronunciations, 97, *100*
  silent letters, 98, *101*
Proper nouns
  possessive forms, 65, 66
  prefixes with, 90
Prophecy/prophesy, 120
Prophet/profit, 112
Publications
  abbreviations used in, 150–51
  capitalization of titles, 136

Quotations, capitalization rules, 129–30

Races, capitalization of, 133
Rain/reign/rein, 113
Rap/wrap, 113
Read/reed, 113
Read/red, 113
Real/reel, 113
Reign/rein/rain, 113
Religious groups, capitalization of, 133
Religious holidays, capitalization of, 138
Right/rite/write, 113
Ring/wring, 113
Road/rode/rowed, 113
Role/roll, 113
Root/route, 113
Rote/wrote, 113
Rowed/road/rode, 113

Sail/sale, 114
Saint, when to abbreviate, 142
Scene/seen, 114
Scent/sent/cent, 106
Schools, capitalization of, 136
School subjects, capitalization rules, 136
Science and technology, spelling list, 162
Sea/see, 114
Seam/seem 114
Seasons, capitalization rules, 137

194 / Mastering Spelling

-sede/-ceed/-cede, 88–89, *92–93*
See/sea, 114
Seed/cede, 106
Seen/scene, 114
Seller/cellar, 106
Sent/scent/cent, 106
Sentences, capitalization rules, 129–30
Sew/so/sow, 114
Sight/site/cite, 106
Signs, forming plurals of, 54
Silent *e*, adding suffixes to words ending in, 31–35, *44*, 74
Silent letters, pronunciation rules, 98, *101*
Singeing/singing, 33
Slang, usage label, 17
Slay/sleigh, 114
So/sow/sew, 114
Soar/sore, 114
Sold/soled, 114
Sole/soul, 114
Some-, words beginning with, 90
Some/sum, 114
Son/sun, 115
Sore/soar, 114
Soul/sole, 114
Sow/sew/so, 114
Spelling
   capitalization, 129–41
   of common prefixes, 85–89, *91–93*
   of compound words, 89–91, *93*
   dictionary aids, 7–15, *22*
   five basic rules, 24–45
   formation of plurals, 46–60
   homonyms and near-homonyms, 102–28
   and pronunciation, 94–101
   use of apostrophes, 61–71
   of words formed from other words, 72–84
Spelling lists
   the arts, 161–62
   British and American spellings, 160–61
   business, 162–63
   politics and government, 163
   problem words, 164–67
   science and technology, 162
Stable/staple, 120
Stair/stare, 115
Stake/steak, 115
States
   abbreviation of, 144–46
   capitalization of, 134
Stationary/stationery, 115
Statue/stature/statute, 121
Steak/stake, 115
Steal/steel, 115
Straight/strait, 115

Street names, capitalization of, 134
Suffixes
   adding to words ending in *c*, 42–43, *45*
   adding to words ending in silent *e*, 31–35, *44*
   adding to words ending in *y*, 28–31, *43–44*
   defined, 24 *fn.*
   that change the form of words, 72–84
   that change to part of speech, 73–80, *82–84*
   when to double consonant before adding, 36–42, *44–45*
Suit/suite, 121
Suite/sweet, 115
Sum/some, 114
Sun/son, 115
Syllables
   accented, 11–12, *20*
   division of, in dictionary entries, 10, *20*
   and doubling rule, 36–42
Synonyms, in dictionary entries, 16, *22*

Tail/tale, 115
Team/teem, 115
Than/then, 121
Threw/through, 115
They're/their/there, 102
Throne/thrown, 115
Tied/tide, 115
Time, apostrophe used to show duration of, 66
Time and events
   abbreviations, 147
   capitalization rules, 137–38
Titles of books and compositions, capitalization rules, 130
Titles of persons
   abbreviation of, 142–43
   capitalization rules, 132
Toe/tow, 116
Told/tolled, 116
Trade names, capitalization of, 136
Trail/trial, 121
Two/to/too, 103

Usage labels, 17–18, *22–23*

Vain/vane/vein, 116
Vale/veil, 116
Verbs
   adjectives formed from, 76–77
   changing nouns to, 75, *82–83*
   changing to nouns, 73–75, *82*
   changing to other word forms, 78–79, *83*
   forming present participle from infinitive, 78–79, *83*

Index / 195

Verbs (*continued*)
   with irregular past tense, 13–14, 20–21
Vial/vile, 116
Volume measures, abbreviations, 148
Vowel sounds, 8–9

Wade/weighed, 116
Wail/whale, 116
Waist/waste, 116
Wait/weight, 116
Wares/wears, 116
Way/weigh, 117
Weak/week, 117
Weather/whether, 117
Weight/wait, 116
Weight measures, abbreviations, 148
Were/where, 121
Whale/wail, 116
Whether/weather, 117

Which/witch, 117
Whine/wine, 117
Whole/hole, 110
Wholly/holy, 110
Whose/who's, 67
Wine/whine, 117
Witch/which, 117
Woman/women, 121
Won/one, 111
Wood/would, 117
Wrap/rap, 113
Wring/ring, 113
Write/right/rite, 113
Wrote/rote, 113

-*y,* words ending in
   adding suffixes to, 28–31, 33, 43–44
   forming plural of, 48–49
You're/your, 102